potatoes
& rice

Simple Cookery

STAR
FIRE

This is a Starfire book
First published in 2001

02 04 05 03

1 3 5 7 9 10 8 6 4 2

Starfire is part of
The Foundry Creative Media Company Limited
Crabtree Hall, Crabtree Lane, Fulham, London, SW6 6TY

Visit the Foundry website: www.foundry.co.uk/recipes

Copyright © The Foundry 2001

ISBN: 1-903817-02-1

The CIP record for this book is available from the British Library.

Printed in Italy

ACKNOWLEDGEMENTS

Authors: Catherine Atkinson, Juliet Barker, Gina Steer, Vicki Smallwood,
Carol Tennant, Mari Mererid Williams and Elizabeth Wolf-Cohen
Editorial Consultant: Gina Steer
Project Editor: Karen Fitzpatrick
Photography: Colin Bowling, Paul Forrester and Stephen Brayne
Home Economists and Stylists: Jacqueline Bellefontaine,
Mandy Phipps, Vicki Smallwood and Penny Stephens
Design Team: Helen Courtney, Jennifer Bishop, Lucy Bradbury and Chris Herbert

All props supplied by Barbara Stewart at Surfaces

NOTE
Recipes using uncooked eggs should be avoided by infants,
the elderly, pregnant women and anyone suffering from an illness.

Special thanks to everyone involved in this book, particularly
Karen Fitzpatrick and Gina Steer.

CONTENTS

SOUPS & STARTERS

FISH

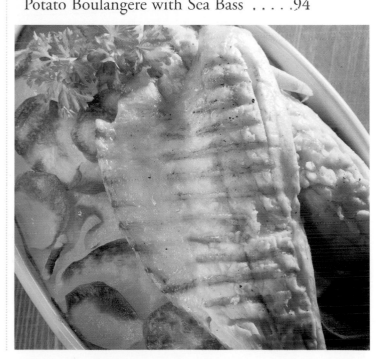

MEAT

POULTRY

VEGETABLES

ENTERTAINING

HYGIENE IN THE KITCHEN

It is well worth remembering that many foods can carry some form of bacteria. In most cases, the worst it will lead to is a bout of food poisoning or gastroenteritis, although for certain groups this can be more serious – the risk can be reduced or eliminated by good food hygiene and proper cooking.

Do not buy food that is past its sell-by date and do not consume any food that is past its use-by date. When buying food, use the eyes and nose. If the food looks tired, limp or a bad colour or it has a rank, acrid or simply bad smell, do not buy or eat it under any circumstances.

Do take special care when preparing raw meat and fish. A separate chopping board should be used for each; wash the knife, board and the hands thoroughly before handling or preparing any other food.

Regularly clean, defrost and clear out the refrigerator or freezer – it is worth checking the packaging to see exactly how long each product is safe to freeze.

Avoid handling food if suffering from an upset stomach as bacteria can be passed through food preparation.

Dish cloths and tea towels must be washed and changed regularly. Ideally use disposable cloths which should be replaced on a daily basis. More durable cloths should be left to soak in bleach, then washed in the washing machine on a boil wash.

Keep the hands, cooking utensils and food preparation surfaces clean and do not allow pets to climb on to any work surfaces.

BUYING

Avoid bulk buying where possible, especially fresh produce such as meat, poultry, fish, fruit and vegetables unless buying for the freezer. Fresh foods lose their nutritional value rapidly so buying a little at a time minimises loss of nutrients. It also eliminates a packed refrigerator which reduces the effectiveness of the refrigeration process.

When buying prepackaged goods such as cans or pots of cream and yogurts, check that the packaging is intact and not damaged or pierced at all. Cans should not be dented, pierced or rusty. Check the sell-by dates even for cans and packets of dry ingredients such as flour and rice. Store fresh foods in the refrigerator as soon as possible – not in the car or the office.

When buying frozen foods, ensure that they are not heavily iced on the outside and the contents feel completely frozen. Ensure that the frozen foods have been stored in the cabinet at the correct storage level and the temperature is below -18°C/-0.4°F. Pack in cool bags to transport home and place in the freezer as soon as possible after purchase.

PREPARATION

Make sure that all work surfaces and utensils are clean and dry. Hygiene should be given priority at all times.

Separate chopping boards should be used for raw and cooked meats, fish and vegetables. Currently, a variety of good-quality plastic boards come in various designs and colours. This makes differentiating easier and the plastic has the added hygienic advantage of being washable at high temperatures in the dishwasher. (NB: If using the board for fish, first wash in cold water, then in hot to prevent odour!) Also, remember that knives and utensils should always be thoroughly cleaned after use.

When cooking, be particularly careful to keep cooked and raw food separate to avoid any contamination. It is worth washing all fruits and vegetables regardless of whether they are going to be eaten raw or lightly cooked. This rule should apply even to prewashed herbs and salads.

Do not reheat food more than once. If using a microwave, always check that the food is piping hot all the way through. (In theory, the food should reach 70°C/158°F and needs to be cooked at that temperature for at least three minutes to ensure that all bacteria are killed.)

All poultry must be thoroughly thawed before using, including chicken and poussin. Remove the food to be thawed from the freezer and place in a shallow dish to contain the juices. Leave the food in the refrigerator until it is completely thawed. A 1.4 kg/3 lb whole chicken will take about 26–30 hours to thaw. To speed up the process immerse the chicken in cold water. However, make sure that the water is changed regularly. When the joints can move freely and no ice crystals remain in the cavity, the bird is completely thawed.

Once thawed, remove the wrapper and pat the chicken dry. Place the chicken in a shallow dish, cover lightly and store as close to the base of the refrigerator as possible. The chicken should be cooked as soon as possible.

Some foods can be cooked from frozen including many prepacked foods such as soups, sauces, casseroles and breads. Where applicable follow the manufacturers' instructions.

Vegetables and fruits can also be cooked from frozen, but meats and fish should be thawed first. The only time food can be refrozen is when the food has been thoroughly thawed then cooked. Once the food has cooled then it can be frozen again. On such occasions the food can only be stored for one month.

All poultry and game (except for duck) must be cooked thoroughly. When cooked the juices will run clear from the thickest part of the bird – the best area to try is usually the thigh. Other meats, like minced meat and pork should be cooked right the way through. Fish should turn opaque, be firm in texture and break easily into large flakes.

When cooking leftovers, make sure they are reheated until piping hot and that any sauce or soup reaches boiling point first.

STORING
REFRIGERATING AND FREEZING

M eat, poultry, fish, seafood and dairy products should all be refrigerated. The temperature of the refrigerator should be between 1–5°C/34–41°F while the freezer temperature should not rise above -18°C/-0.4°F.

To ensure the optimum refrigerator and freezer temperature, avoid leaving the door open for a long time. Try not to overstock the refrigerator as this reduces the airflow inside and affects the effectiveness in cooling the food within.

When refrigerating cooked food, allow it to cool down quickly and completely before refrigerating. Hot food will raise the temperature of the refrigerator and possibly affect or spoil other food stored in it.

Food within the refrigerator and freezer should always be covered. Raw and cooked food should be stored in separate parts of the refrigerator. Cooked food should be kept on the top shelves of the refrigerator, while raw meat, poultry and fish should be placed on bottom shelves to avoid drips and cross-contamination. It is recommended that eggs should be refrigerated in order to maintain their freshness and shelf life.

Take care that frozen foods are not stored in the freezer for too long. Blanched vegetables can be stored for one month; beef, lamb, poultry and pork for six months and unblanched vegetables and fruits in syrup for a year. Oily fish and sausages should be stored for three months. Dairy products can last four to six months while cakes and pastries should be kept in the freezer for three to six months.

HIGH-RISK FOODS

C ertain foods may carry risks to people who are considered vulnerable such as the elderly, the ill, pregnant women, babies, young infants and those suffering from a reccuring illness.

It is advisable to avoid those foods listed below which belong to a higher-risk category.

There is a slight chance that some eggs carry the bacteria salmonella. Cook the eggs until both the yolk and the white are firm to eliminate this risk. Pay particular attention to dishes and products incorporating lightly cooked or raw eggs which should be eliminated from the diet. Sauces including Hollandaise, mayonnaise, mousses, soufflés and meringues all use raw or lightly cooked eggs, as do custard-based dishes, ice creams and sorbets. These are all considered high-risk foods to the vulnerable groups mentioned above.

Certain meats and poultry also carry the potential risk of salmonella and so should be cooked thoroughly until the juices run clear and there is no pinkness left. Unpasteurised products such as milk, cheese (especially soft cheese), pâté, meat (both raw and cooked) all have the potential risk of listeria and should be avoided.

When buying seafood, buy from a reputable source which has a high turnover to ensure freshness. Fish should have bright clear eyes, shiny skin and bright pink or red gills. The fish should feel stiff to the touch, with a slight smell of sea air and iodine. The flesh of fish steaks and fillets should be translucent with no signs of discolouration. Molluscs such as scallops, clams and mussels are sold fresh and are still alive. Avoid any that are open or do not close when tapped lightly. In the same way, univalves such as cockles or winkles should withdraw back into their shells when lightly prodded. When choosing cephalopods such as squid and octopus they should have a firm flesh and pleasant sea smell.

As with all fish, whether it is shellfish or seafish, care is required when freezing it. It is imperative to check whether the fish has been frozen before. If it has been frozen, then it should not be frozen again under any circumstances.

VARIETIES OF POTATOES AND STORAGE

The humble potato is generally taken for granted and the versatility and huge number of varieties of this delicious vegetable are often forgotten. Worldwide there are thousands of different types of potatoes and for about two-thirds of the world, they are the staple food. In this country, almost three-quarters of main crop potatoes are made up of just five varieties. Consumers, however, have gradually become more demanding so a wider range of potatoes suitable for different uses is now available. Although you will still find bags simply labelled 'red' and 'white' in supermarkets, alongside them is also a selection of named varieties. Many of the old varieties of potato are currently being revived, as well as new ones being created.

Potatoes are classified according to how early in the season they are ready for harvesting and are named as follows: first early, second early and main crop. The first earlies are the first new potatoes on the market; they are very fresh and young and the skins can simply be rubbed off. The second earlies are still new potatoes, but their skins will have begun to set. These potatoes will be difficult to scrape and are better cooked in their skins. Main crop potatoes are available all year round and may have been stored for several months. Individual potato varieties have their own characteristics. Some main crop varieties are better for boiling than baking and vice versa, so choose the most appropriate type of potato for the dish being prepared. Check the label, ask your retailer or refer to the list below for guidance.

AILSA (main crop) These medium-sized potatoes are round or oval with white skins and creamy-coloured, floury flesh. Ailsa potatoes are excellent for boiling and chipping.

ANYA (second early) These speciality, knobbly, oval-shaped potatoes have a pinkish skin and white flesh. They have a nutty flavour and waxy texture and are at their best when boiled or used in salads.

ARRAN COMET (first early) These round, and sometimes oval, new potatoes have a white skin and creamy flesh. Large ones are good for chipping.

ARRAN PILOT (first early) The firm flesh of these potatoes makes them an ideal choice for salads. They have white flesh and skins.

ARRAN VICTORY (main crop) These oval-shaped potatoes have a deep purple skin and a bright white flesh. They are the oldest variety of Arran potatoes still available. Arran Victory potatoes have a very floury texture and flavour and are excellent for baking and boiling. Currently they are undergoing a revival – it is well worth seeking this variety out.

ASPERGE (second early) Also known as la ratte and cornichon, these potatoes have a yellow skin and a creamy, very waxy flesh. They are good steamed or boiled and are perfect for salads.

BELLE DE FONTENAY (early main crop) These long potatoes often have a curved shape. Their skins are pale yellow and their flesh is firm, waxy and yellow. They have a wonderful buttery flavour and are particularly good boiled, in salads or mashed.

BINTJE (main crop) With a pale yellow skin and flesh, these potatoes are suitable for all cooking methods and make particularly good chips.

CARA (late main crop) These potatoes may be white or red, round or oval. The flesh is creamy-coloured with a mild flavour and waxy texture. Cara are good all-round potatoes.

CATRIONA (second early) Kidney-shaped potatoes with purple markings around the eyes on the skin and a pale yellow flesh. They have a delicious flavour and are ideal for baking, boiling and mashing.

CHARLOTTE (main crop) Oval or pear-shaped potatoes with pale yellow skin and flesh, a firm, waxy texture and a flavour not unlike chestnuts. They are particulary good boiled, steamed and in salads but can also be baked.

CLEOPATRA (first early) These oval, new potatoes are suitable for boiling, have pink or red skin and a light-yellow, dense flesh.

COLMO (first early) Medium round or oval, these potatoes have a white skin and golden, firm flesh. Their texture and colour make them particularly good for mashing.

DESIREE (main crop) Probably the world's most popular red-skinned potatoes with pale yellow flesh, a firm texture and good flavour. These potatoes are good all-rounders and are great for both mashing and roasting. They also hold their shape well enough for boiling.

DIAMONT (main crop) These potatoes were a common and popular variety in the 1930s and are still available now. They are long and oval shaped with a rough, white skin and a firm, waxy yellow interior. Their flavour is slightly sharp and nutty.

DUKE OF YORK (first early) These long, oval new potatoes have a sweet flavour, firm texture, pale creamy skins and light yellow flesh. A red-skinned variety is also available.

EPICURE (first early) Round potatoes with white or sometimes pink-tinged skin, creamy, firm flesh and a distinctive flavour. Suitable for both boiling and baking.

ESTIMA (second early) Oval-shaped potatoes with a light yellow skin and flesh. Their firm, moist texture and subtle flavour make them good baking potatoes. These potatoes were the first yellow-fleshed potatoes to become popular.

GOLDEN WONDER (late main crop) These large, oval potatoes have a dark, russet-coloured skin and light yellow flesh. They are excellent for baking and their floury texture makes them especially good for crisps.

HOME GUARD (first early) Round or slightly oval, with white skins and creamy-coloured flesh, these potatoes have a dry, floury texture and a good flavour with slightly bitter overtones. These potatoes are ideal for boiling, roasting and chipping. They were a favourite during the Second World War and are one of the first varieties of new potatoes available.

JERSEY ROYALS (second early) The best and most popular new potatoes, Jersey Royals have a creamy-coloured skin and flesh and can be served both hot or cold. When cooked (boiled or steamed), they are tender rather than firm and are best served whole, with or without the skins.

KERR'S PINK (late main crop) Round, pink-skinned potatoes with creamy-white flesh and a floury texture, these potatoes are suitable for boiling, baking, mashing, roasting and chipping.

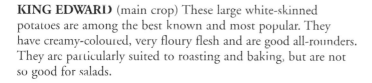

KING EDWARD (main crop) These large white-skinned potatoes are among the best known and most popular. They have creamy-coloured, very floury flesh and are good all-rounders. They are particularly suited to roasting and baking, but are not so good for salads.

MARFONA (second early) These are good baking potatoes, also suitable for boiling, but not for roasting.

MARIS BARD (first early) These white-skinned potatoes have firm, waxy flesh with a slightly earthy taste. They are good for boiling and suitable for most other methods. They should be avoided, however, late in the season when they lose their flavour and are in danger of disintegrating during cooking.

MARIS PEER (second early) These potatoes have white flesh and skins with an excellent flavour. They are good for salads as well as boiling and steaming.

MORAG (main crop) These potatoes have a pale skin and a white, waxy flesh. Serve them boiled, steamed or baked.

NADINE (second early) These potatoes are available in two sizes. There are the small new potatoes and the slightly larger-sized potatoes which are suitable for baking. Nadine potatoes have creamy-yellow skins and white, waxy flesh, but their flavour is somewhat bland.

PENTLAND JAVELIN (first early) These new potatoes have very white, smooth skins and milky-white flesh. These potatoes are ideal for salads, but are also good boiled or steamed.

PENTLAND SQUIRE (main crop) Usually white skinned, but occasionally russet, the flesh of these potatoes is very white. Their floury texture makes them perfect for baking. They are also good for boiling and mashing, but are poor in salads.

PINK FIR APPLE (main crop) These knobbly, misshapen potatoes have white skins with a pinkish blush and a pale yellow flesh. They are firm and waxy with a delicious nutty flavour and have many of the characteristics of new potatoes. They are best cooked in their skins as their shape makes them extremely difficult to peel and are good steamed, boiled and served cold in salads.

SHELAGH (main crop) This Scottish variety has a creamy flesh and pinkish patches all over the skin. The waxy texture of these potatoes makes them good for boiling, steaming or chipping.

WILJA (second early) These potatoes have pale yellow skins and flesh. They are good, flavoursome all-rounders and hold their shape when cooked, so are particularly suitable for salads, boiling and steaming. They can also be used for baking and roasting.

SWEET POTATOES These potatoes are imported from tropical areas of the Americas and from many other hot countries around the world. Their skins are red and the flesh inside is either white or orange. Orange-fleshed sweet potatoes have a denser, waxier texture and tend to hold their shape better, whereas white-fleshed ones are starchier and not quite as sugary. It is impossible to tell from the outside what colour the flesh will be within, so unless labelled you may need to scrape off a small patch of skin. Treat in much the same way as ordinary potatoes – bake, mash or fry.

BUYING AND STORAGE

When buying potatoes always choose ones with smooth, firm skins. When purchasing new potatoes, check that they are really young and fresh by scraping the skin – it should peel away very easily. Only buy the quantity you need and use within a couple of days. Check main crop potatoes to make sure that they are firm and not sprouting or showing any signs of mould. Avoid buying and discard any potatoes with greenish patches or carefully cut them out. These parts of the potato are toxic and a sign that they have been stored in light.

Potatoes should be stored in a cool, dark place but not in the refrigerator as the dampness will make them sweat, causing mould to grow. If the potatoes come in plastic bags, take them out and store in a paper bag or on a vegetable rack. If you prefer to buy in bulk, keep the potatoes in a cold, dark, dry place such as a larder or garage, making sure that they do not freeze in cold weather.

Sweet potatoes should be stored in a cool, dry place, but unlike ordinary potatoes, do not need to be kept in the dark.

VARIETIES OF RICE AND STORAGE

R ice is the staple food of many countries throughout the world. Every country and culture has its own repertoire of rice recipes, for example, India has the aromatic biryani, Spain has the saffron-scented paella and Italy has the creamy risotto. Rice is grown on marshy, flooded land where other cereals cannot thrive and because it is grown in so many different areas, there is a huge range of rice types.

LONG-GRAIN WHITE RICE This is probably the most widely used type of rice. Long-grain white rice has been milled so that the husk, bran and germ is removed. If you buy it loose, it is sometimes whitened with chalk or other substances, so thorough rinsing under cold running water is essential. Easy-cook long-grain white rice has been steamed under pressure before milling. This makes it difficult to over-cook, therefore separate dry and fluffy grains are virtually guaranteed. Precooked rice, also known as parboiled or converted rice, is polished white rice which is half cooked after milling, then dried again. It is quick and simple to cook, but has a rather bland flavour. Java rice is one of the slightly shorter long-grain rices and because it is particularly absorbent is often used in baked rice dishes.

Rice is sometimes referred to by the country or region in which it was originally grown. Patna rice is a term used to describe a type of long-grain rice which originated from Patna in north-east India. Long-grain rice is rarely labelled by country of origin, as it now mostly comes from America. Carolina is simply another name for long-grain rice and refers to the region in America where rice was first planted.

LONG-GRAIN BROWN RICE Here the outer husk is removed, leaving the bran and germ behind, so retaining a lot more of the fibre, vitamins and minerals. It has a nutty, slightly chewy texture and because it is less refined takes longer to cook than long-grain white rice.

BASMATI RICE This slender long-grain rice, which may be white or brown, is grown in the foothills of the Himalayas. After harvesting, it is allowed to mature for a year, giving it a unique aromatic flavour, hence its name which means fragrant. Its perfect, separate, white and fluffy grains frequently feature in Indian cooking.

RISOTTO RICE Grown in the north of Italy, this is the only rice that is suitable for making Italian risotto. The grains are plump and stubby and have the ability to absorb large quantities of liquid without becoming too soft, cooking to a creamy texture with a slight bite. The starchiness of risotto rice makes it a good addition to soups where it acts as thickener. It can also be made into moulded rice dishes such as timbales, as the grains hold together without being too sticky. There are two grades of risotto rice, superfino and fino. Arborio rice is the most widely sold variety of the former, but you may also find carnaroli, Roma and baldo in Italian food shops and delicatessens. Fino rice, such as vialone nano has a slightly shorter grain, but the flavour is still excellent.

VALENCIA RICE Traditionally used for Spanish paella, Valencia rice is soft and tender when ready. The medium-sized grains break down easily, so should be left unstirred during cooking to absorb the flavour of the stock and other ingredients.

JASMINE RICE Also known as Thai fragrant rice, this long-grain rice has a delicate, almost perfumed aroma and flavour and has a soft, sticky texture.

GLUTINOUS RICE White or black (unpolished), these short grains are high in starch and feature in Chinese and Japanese cooking, as the grains stick together when cooked, making them easy to eat with chopsticks. This rice has a slightly sweet taste and is used for making dim sum as well as sweet, sticky puddings.

JAPANESE SUSHI RICE This is similar to glutinous rice in that it has a sticky texture. When mixed with rice vinegar it is easy to roll up with a filling inside to make sushi. Much of the sushi rice eaten in the West is now grown in California.

PUDDING RICE This rounded, short-grain rice is ideal for puddings and rice desserts. The grains swell

RICE PRODUCTS

Numerous Japanese ingredients are made from rice. Japan's national drink, sake, is a spirit distilled from rice and is often used in cooking. Mirin is a sweet rice wine used as a marinade in dishes such as teriyaki. Rice vinegar is made from soured and fermented wine. Japanese rice vinegar has a soft, mellow flavour, whereas Chinese rice vinegar has a very sharp taste.

Sometimes Japanese rice vinegars are made into flavoured vinegars by mixing the vinegar with soy sauce, for example, to make dashi. Most rice vinegars are a clear, pale golden colour, but brown rice vinegar, made from wholegrain rice, is deep brown.

Amasake is a rice drink, often sold in healthfood stores and is made by adding enzymes to wholegrain pudding rice. It can be used in puddings and baking as an alternative to milk.

Rice paper is made from a mixture of rice flour, salt and water. Machines roll the mixture out until it is extremely thin and transparent, then it is dried out. Rice paper comes in hard circles or triangles and is easily softened by placing between two dampened tea towels. When soft, the rice paper can be wrapped around a filling, then steamed or fried, to make dishes such as pancake rolls or dim sum.

and absorb large quantities of milk during cooking, giving puddings a rich and soft creamy consistency. Brown pudding rice is also available.

RED RICE This is grown in small amounts in the Camargue, a marshy region in Provence in France. It is similar to brown rice in taste and texture, but when cooked its red colour develops, making it an attractive addition to salads and other rice dishes.

WILD RICE Strictly speaking this is an aquatic grass which is grown in North America rather than a true variety of rice. Some wild rice is now grown commercially, which has reduced the price a little, but much of it is still found growing wild in North America's vast lakes, where only native Americans have the right to gather it. The black grains are long and slender and after harvesting and cleaning are toasted to remove the chaff and intensify the nutty flavour and slight chewiness. Although wild rice is much more expensive than other rices, a small quantity goes a long way – it is often sold as a mixture with either long-grain white or basmati rice.

FLAKED RICE White or brown rice grains are steamed and rolled to paper thinness to make flaked rice. It is extremely quick to cook and is mainly used to make creamy puddings, but may also be used for baking. It is sometimes found in commercially made muesli mixtures.

GROUND RICE This type of rice is made by grounding white rice to the size of fine sand. Like flaked rice, it can be used to make fast rice puddings and is also frequently used in baking, especially for making biscuits such as shortbread.

RICE FLOUR Raw rice can be ground finely to make rice flour which may be used to thicken sauces (you need about 1 tablespoon to thicken 300 ml/½ pint of liquid) or as a vital ingredient in sticky Asian cakes and desserts. It is also used to make fresh and dried rice noodles. When rice flour is ground even more finely, it becomes rice powder and has a fine consistency like cornflour. It can be found in Asian food stores.

BUYING AND STORING RICE

Rice will keep for several years if kept in sealed packets, however, it is at its best when fresh. To ensure freshness, always buy rice from reputable shops with a good turnover and buy in small quantities. Once opened, store the rice in an airtight container in a cool, dry place to keep out moisture. Most rices (but not risotto) benefit from washing before cooking – tip into a sieve and rinse under cold running water for a minute or so, until the water runs clear.

Cooked rice will keep well for up to two days if cooled rapidly and stored in a bowl covered with clingfilm in the refrigerator. If eating rice cold, serve within 24 hours – after this time it should be reheated thoroughly. To reheat rice, place it in a heavy-based saucepan with 2–3 tablespoons of water, cover and heat until piping hot, shaking the pan occasionally. Alternatively, reheat the bowl of cooled rice in the microwave, piercing the clingfilm first.

COOKING TECHNIQUES FOR POTATOES

Generally, new potato varieties have a firm and waxy texture that do not break up during cooking, so are ideal for boiling, steaming and salads. Main crop potatoes, on the other hand, have a more floury texture and lend themselves to mashing and roasting – both types are suitable for chips. When cooking potatoes, it is important to make sure the potatoes that you are using are the correct type for the dish being prepared. Whichever way you choose to serve potatoes, allow 175–225 g/6–8 oz per person.

BOILING POTATOES

NEW POTATOES

Most of the new potatoes available nowadays are fairly clean – especially those sold in supermarkets – and simply need a light scrub before cooking in their skins. If the potatoes are very dirty, use a small scrubbing brush or scourer to remove both the skins and dirt. Add them to a pan of cold, salted water and bring to the boil. Cover the pan with a lid and simmer for 12–15 minutes or until tender. Add a couple of sprigs of fresh herbs to the pan if you like – fresh mint is traditionally used to flavour potatoes. Drain the potatoes thoroughly and serve hot, tossed in a little melted butter or for a change a tablespoon of pesto. The skins of first early new potatoes will peel away easily, but second earlies should be served in their skins or peeled when cooked (hold the hot potatoes with a fork to make this easier). Very firm new potatoes can be added to boiling water, simmered for 8 minutes, and then left to stand in the hot water for a further 10 minutes until cooked through.

OLD POTATOES

Choose a main crop potato suitable for boiling, then thinly peel and cut into even-sized pieces. Add to a saucepan of cold, salted water and bring to the boil. Cover the pan with a lid and simmer for 20 minutes or until tender.

Alternatively, you can cook the potatoes in their skins and peel them after cooking. (It is particularly important to cook floury potatoes gently or the outsides may start to fall apart before they are tender in the centre. Drain the potatoes in a colander, then return them to the pan to dry out over a very low heat for 1–2 minutes.) If you are planning to serve the potatoes mashed, roughly mash them and add a knob of butter and 2 tablespoons of milk per person. Mash until smooth, either with a hand masher, mouli grater or a potato ricer. Season to taste with salt, freshly ground black pepper and a little freshly grated nutmeg if liked, then beat for a few seconds with a wooden spoon until fluffy. As an alternative to butter, use a good-quality olive oil or crème fraîche. Finely chopped red and green chillies, crispy-cooked crumbled bacon, fresh herbs or grated Parmesan cheese can also be stirred in for additional flavour.

STEAMING POTATOES

All potatoes are suitable for steaming. Floury potatoes, however, are ideal for this method of cooking as they fall apart easily.

New and small potatoes can be steamed whole, but larger ones should be cut into even-sized pieces. Place the potatoes in a steamer, colander or sieve over boiling water and cover. Steam for 10 minutes if the potatoes are very small or if they are cut into large chunks cook for 20–25 minutes.

FRYING POTATOES

CHIPPED POTATOES

To make chipped potatoes (commonly known as chips), wash, peel and cut the potatoes into 1.5 cm/⅝ inch slices. Cut the slices into long strips about 1.5 cm/⅝ inches wide. Place the strips in a bowl of cold water and leave for 20 minutes, then drain and dry well on kitchen paper – moisture will make the fat spit. Pour some oil into a deep, heavy-based saucepan or deep-fat fryer, making sure that the oil does not go any further than halfway up the sides of the pan. Heat the oil to 190°C/375°F, or until a chip dropped into the fat rises to the surface straight away and is surrounded by bubbles. Put the chips into a wire basket and lower into the oil and cook for 7–8 minutes or until golden. Remove and increase the heat of the oil to 200°C/400°F. Lower the chips into the oil again and cook for 2–3 minutes, or until they are crisp and golden brown. Drain on kitchen paper before serving.

Slightly finer chips are known as pommes frites, even finer ones as pommes allumettes and the finest of all as pommes pailles (straw chips). Paper-thin slices of peeled potatoes, cut with a sharp knife or using a mandoline or food processor, can be deep-fried a few at a time to make crisps or game chips.

To make lower-fat chips, preheat the oven to 200°C/ 400°F/Gas Mark 6 and place a non-stick baking tray in the oven to heat up. Cut the potatoes into chips as above or into chunky wedges, if preferred. Put the chips or wedges in a pan of cold water and quickly bring to the boil. Simmer for 2 minutes, then drain in a colander. Leave for a few minutes to dry, then drizzle over 1½–2 tablespoons of olive or sunflower oil and toss to coat. Tip on to the heated baking tray and cook in the preheated oven for 20–25 minutes, turning occasionally until golden brown and crisp.

SAUTÉED POTATOES

Cut peeled potatoes into rounds about 0.5 cm/¼ inch thick and pat dry. Heat 25 g/1 oz unsalted butter and 2 tablespoons of oil in a large, heavy-based frying pan until hot. Add the potatoes in a single layer and cook for 4–5 minutes until the undersides are golden. Turn with a large fish slice and cook the other side until golden and tender. Drain on kitchen paper and sprinkle with a little salt before serving.

BAKING POTATOES

Allow a 300–350 g/11–12 oz potato per person and choose a variety such as Maris Piper, Cara or King Edward. Wash and dry the potatoes, prick the skins lightly, then rub each one with a little oil and sprinkle with salt. Bake at 200°C/400°F/Gas Mark 6 for 1–1½ hours or until the skins are crisp and the centres are very soft. To speed up the cooking time, thread on to metal skewers as this conducts heat to the middle of the potatoes.

ROASTING POTATOES

For crisp and brown outsides and fluffy centres choose potatoes suitable for baking. Thinly peel the potatoes and cut into even-sized pieces. Drop them into a pan of boiling, salted water and simmer for 5 minutes. Turn off the heat and leave for a further 3–4 minutes. Drain well and return the potatoes to the pan over a low heat for a minute to dry them and to roughen the edges. Carefully transfer them to a roasting tin containing hot oil or dripping. Baste well, then bake at 220°C/425°F/Gas Mark 7 for 20 minutes. Turn them and cook for a further 20–30 minutes, turning and basting at least one more time. Serve as soon as the potatoes are ready.

POTATO CROQUETTES

Mash dry, boiled potatoes with just a little butter or olive oil, then stir in 1 egg yolk mixed with 1–2 tablespoons of milk or crème fraîche to make a firm mixture. Shape the mashed potatoes into small cylinders about 5 cm/2 inches long, rolling them in flour. Dip in beaten egg and then in fresh, white breadcrumbs. Chill the croquettes in the refrigerator for 30 minutes. Place a little unsalted butter and oil in a heavy-based frying pan and slowly heat until the butter has melted. Shallow fry the croquettes, turning occasionally until they are golden brown and crisp.

ROSTI

Parboil peeled, waxy potatoes in boiling, salted water for 8 minutes, drain and leave to cool before coarsely grating into a bowl. Season well with salt and freshly ground black pepper and freshly chopped herbs if liked. Heat a mixture of unsalted butter and oil in a heavy-based frying pan until bubbling. Add tablespoonfuls of the grated potato into the pan and flatten with the back of a fish slice. Cook over a medium heat for about 7 minutes or until crisp and golden. Turn and cook the other side.

COOKING POTATOES IN A CLAY POT

Terracotta potato pots can cook up to 450 g/1 lb of whole potatoes at a time. Soak the clay pot for at least 20 minutes before use, then add even-sized, preferably smallish potatoes. Drizzle over a little olive oil and season generously with salt and freshly ground black pepper. Cover the pot with the lid and put in a cold oven, setting the temperature to 200°C/400°F/Gas Mark 6. The potatoes will take about 45 minutes to cook.

MICROWAVED POTATOES

This method of cooking is suitable for boiling and baking potatoes, providing you do not want the skins to be crispy. To cook new potatoes, prick the skins with a skewer to prevent them from bursting, then place in a bowl with 3 tablespoons of boiling water. Cover with clingfilm which has been pierced two or three times and cook on High for 12–15 minutes, or until tender. Peeled chunks of potato can be cooked in the same way. To bake potatoes, place each potato on a circle of kitchen paper. Make several cuts in each to ensure that the skins do not burst. Transfer to the microwave plate and cook on High for 4–6 minutes per potato, allowing an extra 3–4 minutes for every additional potato. Turn the potatoes at least once during cooking. Leave to stand for 5 minutes before serving.

HEALTH AND NUTRITION

Potatoes are high in complex carbohydrates, providing sustained energy. They are also an excellent source of vitamins B and C and minerals such as iron and potassium. They contain almost no fat and are high in dietary fibre.

COOKING TECHNIQUES FOR RICE

There are countless ways to cook rice and there are even more opinions about how to do so! Much of course, depends on the variety and brand of rice being used, the dish being prepared and the desired results. Each variety of rice has its own characteristics. Some types of rice cook to light, separate grains; some to a rich, creamy consistency and some to a consistency where the grains stick together. It is important, therefore, to ensure that the appropriate rice is used. Different types of rice have very different powers of absorption. Long-grain rice will absorb about three times its weight in water, whereas just 25 g/1 oz of plump and short-grained pudding rice can soak up a massive 300 ml/½ pint of liquid.

COOKING LONG-GRAIN RICE

By far the simplest method of cooking long-grain rice – whether white, brown or basmati – is to add it to plenty of boiling, salted water in a large saucepan, so that the rice grains can move freely and do not stick together. Allow about 50 g/2 oz of rice per person when cooking as an accompaniment. Rinse it under cold, running water until clear – this removes any starch still clinging to the grains – then tip into the rapidly boiling water. Stir once, then when the water comes back to the boil, turn down the heat a little and simmer uncovered, allowing 10–12 minutes for white rice and 30–40 minutes for brown (check the packet timings, as brands of rice vary). The easiest way to test if the rice is cooked is to bite a couple of grains – they should be tender but still firm. Drain the rice straight away, then return to the pan with a little butter and herbs if liked. Fluff the grains with a fork and serve. If you need to keep the rice warm, put it in a bowl and place over a pan of barely simmering water. Cover the top of the bowl with a clean tea towel until ready to serve.

ABSORPTION METHOD

Cooking rice using the absorption method is also very simple and is favoured by many because no draining is involved and therefore no water is wasted. Also, by using this method, stock and other flavourful ingredients can be added and will be absorbed by the rice. Furthermore, valuable nutrients are retained that would otherwise be lost in the cooking water when drained. To cook rice this way, weigh out the quantity of rice you require, then measure it by volume in a measuring jug – you will need about 150 ml/¼ pint for 2 people. Briefly rinse the rice in a sieve under cold running water, then tip into a large heavy-based saucepan. If liked, you can cook the rice in a little butter or oil for about 1 minute. Pour in two parts water to one part rice (or use stock if you prefer), season with salt and bring to the boil uncovered. Cover the pan with a tight-fitting lid, then simmer gently without lifting the lid, until the liquid is absorbed and the rice is tender. White rice will take 15 minutes to cook, whereas brown rice will take about 35 minutes. It is important to simmer over a very low heat or the liquid will cook away before the rice is ready. Do not be tempted to check the rice too often while it is cooking as you will let out steam and therefore moisture. If there is still a little liquid

left when the rice is tender, remove the lid and cook for about a minute until evaporated. Remove from the heat and leave to stand with the lid on for 4–5 minutes. Do not rinse the rice when it is cooked, just fluff up with a fork before serving. This method is also good for cooking Jasmine and Valencia rice.

OVEN-BAKED METHOD

The oven-baked method also works by absorption. It takes a little longer than cooking rice on the hob, but is ideal to add to the oven if you are roasting or simmering a casserole.

To make oven-baked rice for two people, gently fry a chopped onion in 1 tablespoon of olive oil in a 1.1 litre/ 2 pint flameproof casserole until soft and golden (leave the onion out if preferred). Add 75 g/3 oz long-grain rice and cook for 1 minute, then stir in 300 ml/½ pint of stock – you can also add a finely pared strip of lemon rind or a bay leaf at this stage. Cover with a lid or tinfoil and bake on the middle shelf of a preheated oven at 180°C/ 350°F/Gas Mark 4 for 40 minutes, or until the rice is tender and all the stock has been absorbed. Fluff up with a fork before serving.

COOKING IN THE MICROWAVE

Rinse long-grain white or brown rice in cold running water, then place in a large heat-proof bowl. Add boiling water or stock to the bowl, allowing 300 ml/½ pint for 125 g/4 oz rice and 550 ml/18 fl oz for 225 g/8 oz rice. Add a pinch of salt and a knob of butter, if desired. Cover with clingfilm, making a few air holes to allow the steam to escape and microwave on High for 3 minutes. Stir, then re-cover and microwave on Medium for 12 minutes for white rice and 25 minutes for brown. Leave to stand, covered, for 5 minutes before fluffing up with a fork and serving.

IN A PRESSURE COOKER

Follow the quantities given for the absorption method and bring to the boil in the pressure cooker. Stir once, cover with the lid and bring to a high 6.8 kg/15 lb pressure. Lower the heat and cook for 5 minutes if white rice or cook for 8 minutes if brown rice.

IN A RICE COOKER

Follow the quantities given for the absorption method. Put the rice, salt and boiling water or stock in the cooker, bring back to the boil and cover. When all the liquid has been absorbed the cooker will turn itself off automatically.

WILD RICE

This type of rice can be cooked by any of the methods used for long-grain rice, however the cooking time required is longer. It will take between 35–50 minutes to cook wild rice, depending on whether you like your rice slightly chewy or very tender. To speed up the cooking time, by 5–10 minutes, soak the rice in cold water first for 30 minutes. This also increases the volume of the rice when it is cooked.

RED RICE

Cook this in the same way as brown rice as this type of rice has a very hard grain. It is best to cook the rice for about 40–60 minutes if you like your rice really tender – it will still keep its shape.

RISOTTO RICE

Most rices should not be stirred during cooking as it breaks up the grains and makes them soggy. Risotto rice is different as it can absorb nearly five times its weight in liquid and still retains its shape. A good risotto has a creamy texture, with a slight bite to the individual grains and is made by adding the cooking liquid gradually and stirring almost continuously during cooking.

For a classic risotto (known as alla Milanese) for four people, place 1 tablespoon of olive oil and a knob of butter in a large heavy-based saucepan. Slowly heat the butter and oil until the butter has melted. Add 1 chopped onion to the pan and cook until tender. Add 150 ml/¼ pint of dry white wine and boil rapidly until almost totally reduced. Stir in 300 g/11 oz risotto rice. Add 1 litre/³⁄₄ pints boiling vegetable or chicken stock, a ladleful at a time – each ladleful should be completely absorbed by the rice before the next one is added. Continue adding the stock until the rice is tender. This will take 15–20 minutes. (It may not be necessary to add all of the stock to achieve the desired consistency.) Serve the risotto straight away, sprinkled with grated Parmesan cheese. The basic risotto can be flavoured in many ways. Try adding a couple of bay leaves, or a lemon grass stalk, or a large pinch of saffron to the stock or use more red or white wine and less stock.

GLUTINOUS RICE

This rice is steamed (instead of being cooked in boiling water), until the grains are soft, tender and stick together in a mass. Cooking times vary slightly according to the brand, so check the packet instructions for specific directions.

PUDDING RICE

For a simple rice pudding put 50 g/2 oz of pudding rice in a buttered 1.2 litre/2 pint oven-proof dish with sugar to taste. Pour over 600 ml/1 pint of near-boiling milk and bake in a preheated oven at 150°C/300°F/Gas Mark 2 for 30 minutes. Stir, then bake for a further 1–1¼ hours until tender. Vary the flavour by infusing the milk with orange rind, or add nuts and dried fruit to the mixture or use 300 ml/½ pint coconut milk or single cream and 300 ml/½ pint of milk instead of milk alone.

HEALTH AND NUTRITION

Rice has been the dietary staple of the East for centuries where it has provided a healthy, balanced diet and has added substance to the small quantities of meat used in Eastern cooking. It is low in fat and high in complex carbohydrates which are absorbed slowly, so help to maintain blood sugar levels. Rice is also a reasonable source of protein and provides most of the B vitamins and the minerals potassium and phosphorus. It is also a gluten-free cereal, making it suitable for coeliacs. Like other unrefined grains, brown rice is richer in nutrients and fibre than refined white rice.

SWEDE, TURNIP, PARSNIP & POTATO SOUP

INGREDIENTS   Serves 4

2 large onions, peeled
25 g/1 oz butter
2 medium carrots, peeled and
  roughly chopped
175 g/6 oz swede, peeled and
  roughly chopped
125 g/4 oz turnip, peeled and
  roughly chopped
125 g/4 oz parsnips, peeled
  and roughly chopped

175 g/6 oz potatoes, peeled
1 litre/1¾ pints vegetable stock
½ tsp freshly grated nutmeg
salt and freshly ground black
  pepper
4 tbsp vegetable oil, for frying
125 ml/4 fl oz double cream
warm crusty bread, to serve

1 Finely chop 1 onion. Melt the butter in a large saucepan and add the onion, carrots, swede, turnip, parsnip and potatoes. Cover and cook gently for about 10 minutes, without colouring. Stir occasionally during this time.

2 Add the stock and season to taste with the nutmeg, salt and pepper. Cover and bring to the boil, then reduce the heat and simmer gently for 15–20 minutes, or until the vegetables are tender. Remove from the heat and leave to cool for 30 minutes.

3 Heat the oil in a large heavy-based frying pan. Add the onions and cook over a medium heat, for about 2–3 minutes, stirring frequently, until golden brown. Remove the onions with a slotted spoon and drain well on absorbent kitchen paper. As they cool, they will turn crispy.

4 Pour the cooled soup into a food processor or blender and process to form a smooth purée. Return to the cleaned pan, adjust the seasoning, then stir in the cream. Gently reheat and top with the crispy onions. Serve immediately with chunks of bread.

HELPFUL HINT

For a lower-fat version of this delicious soup, add milk (skimmed if preferred) rather than cream when reheating.

POTATO & FENNEL SOUP

INGREDIENTS   Serves 4

25 g/1 oz butter
2 large onions, peeled and
   thinly sliced
2–3 garlic cloves, peeled and
   crushed
1 tsp salt
2 medium potatoes (about
   450 g/1 lb in weight), peeled
   and diced

1 fennel bulb, trimmed and
   finely chopped
½ tsp caraway seeds
1 litre/1¾ pints vegetable stock
freshly ground black pepper
2 tbsp freshly chopped parsley
4 tbsp crème fraîche
roughly torn pieces of French
   stick, to serve

1 Melt the butter in a large heavy-based saucepan. Add the onions, with the garlic and half the salt, and cook over a medium heat, stirring occasionally, for 7–10 minutes, or until the onions are very soft and beginning to turn brown.

2 Add the potatoes, fennel bulb, caraway seeds and the remaining salt. Cook for about 5 minutes, then pour in the vegetable stock. Bring to the boil, partially cover and simmer for 15–20 minutes, or until the potatoes are tender. Stir in the chopped parsley and adjust the seasoning to taste.

3 For a smooth-textured soup, allow to cool slightly then pour into a food processor or blender and blend until smooth. Reheat the soup gently, then ladle into individual soup bowls. For a chunky soup, omit this blending stage and ladle straight from the saucepan into soup bowls.

4 Swirl a spoonful of crème fraîche into each bowl and serve immediately with roughly-torn pieces of French stick.

FOOD FACT

A fennel bulb is in fact the swollen stem of a plant known as Florence fennel. Originating in Italy, Florence fennel has a distinct aniseed flavour, which mellows and sweetens when cooked. Look out for well-rounded bulbs with bright green fronds. Fennel is at its best when fresh, so should be used as soon as possible after buying. It may be stored in the salad drawer of the refrigerator for a few days.

CAWL

INGREDIENTS
Serves 4–6

700 g/1½ lb scrag end of lamb
or best end of neck chops
pinch of salt
2 large onions, peeled and
thinly sliced
3 large potatoes, peeled and
cut into chunks
2 parsnips, peeled and cut
into chunks

1 swede, peeled and cut into
chunks
3 large carrots, peeled and cut
into chunks
2 leeks, trimmed and sliced
freshly ground black pepper
4 tbsp freshly chopped parsley
warm crusty bread, to serve

1 Put the lamb in a large
saucepan, cover with cold
water and bring to the boil. Add
a generous pinch of salt. Simmer
gently for 1½ hours, then set aside
to cool completely, preferably
overnight.

2 The next day, skim the fat off
the surface of the lamb liquid
and discard. Return the saucepan
to the heat and bring back to the
boil. Simmer for 5 minutes. Add
the onions, potatoes, parsnips,
swede and carrots and return to
the boil. Reduce the heat, cover
and cook for about 20 minutes,
stirring occasionally.

3 Add the leeks and season
to taste with salt and pepper.
Cook for a further 10 minutes, or
until all the vegetables are tender.

4 Using a slotted spoon, remove
the meat from the saucepan
and take the meat off the bone.
Discard the bones and any gristle,
then return the meat to the pan.

Adjust the seasoning to taste,
stir in the parsley, then serve
immediately with plenty of
warm crusty bread.

FOOD FACT

Many traditional Welsh
recipes such as Cawl feature
lamb. This flavoursome soup
was once a staple dish, originally made with scraps of
mutton or lamb and vegetables cooked together in a
broth. Use Welsh lamb if
possible for this modern
version. The meat is lean and
tender and may have the
delicate flavour of herbs if the
sheep have been grazing on
the wild thyme and rosemary
that grow in the mountains.

POTATOES, LEEK & ROSEMARY SOUP

INGREDIENTS — Serves 4

50 g/2 oz butter
450 g/1 lb leeks, trimmed and finely sliced
700 g/1½ lb potatoes, peeled and roughly chopped
900 ml/1½ pints vegetable stock
4 sprigs of fresh rosemary

450 ml/¾ pint full-cream milk
2 tbsp freshly chopped parsley
2 tbsp crème fraîche
salt and freshly ground black pepper
wholemeal rolls, to serve

1 Melt the butter in a large saucepan, add the leeks and cook gently for 5 minutes, stirring frequently. Remove 1 tablespoon of the cooked leeks and reserve for garnishing.

2 Add the potatoes, vegetable stock, rosemary sprigs and milk. Bring to the boil, then reduce the heat, cover and simmer gently for 20–25 minutes, or until the vegetables are tender.

3 Cool for 10 minutes. Discard the rosemary, then pour into a food processor or blender and blend well to form a smooth-textured soup.

4 Return the soup to the cleaned saucepan and stir in the chopped parsley and crème fraîche. Season to taste with salt and pepper. If the soup is too thick, stir in a little more milk or water. Reheat gently without boiling, then ladle into warm soup bowls. Garnish the soup with the reserved leeks and serve immediately with wholemeal rolls.

TASTY TIP

This rosemary-scented version of vichyssoise is equally delicious served cold. Allow the soup to cool before covering, then chill in the refrigerator for at least 2 hours. The soup will thicken as it chills, so you may need to thin it to the desired consistency with more milk or stock and season before serving. It is important to use fresh rosemary rather than dried for this recipe. If unavailable, use 2 bay leaves, or add a bruised fresh lemon grass stalk for a delicate flavour.

CREAM OF SPINACH SOUP

INGREDIENTS

Serves 6–8

1 large onion, peeled and
  chopped
5 large plump garlic cloves,
  peeled and chopped
2 medium potatoes, peeled
  and chopped
750 ml/1¼ pints cold water
1 tsp salt
450 g/1 lb spinach, washed
  and large stems removed

50 g/2 oz butter
3 tbsp flour
750 ml/1¼ pints milk
½ tsp freshly grated nutmeg
freshly ground black pepper
6–8 tbsp crème fraîche or
  soured cream
warm foccacia bread, to serve

1 Place the onion, garlic and potatoes in a large saucepan and cover with the cold water. Add half the salt and bring to the boil. Cover and simmer for 15–20 minutes, or until the potatoes are tender. Remove from the heat and add the spinach. Cover and set aside for 10 minutes.

2 Slowly melt the butter in another saucepan, add the flour and cook over a low heat for about 2 minutes. Remove the saucepan from the heat and add the milk, a little at a time, stirring continuously. Return to the heat and cook, stirring continuously, for 5–8 minutes, or until the sauce is smooth and slightly thickened. Add the freshly grated nutmeg, or to taste.

3 Blend the cooled potato and spinach mixture in a food processor or blender to a smooth purée, then return to the saucepan and gradually stir in the white

sauce. Season to taste with salt and pepper and gently reheat, taking care not to allow the soup to boil. Ladle into soup bowls and top with spoonfuls of crème fraîche or soured cream. Serve immediately with warm foccacia bread.

HELPFUL HINT

When choosing spinach, always look for fresh, crisp, dark green leaves. Use within 1–2 days of buying and store in a cool place until needed. To prepare, wash in several changes of water to remove any dirt or grit and shake off as much excess water as possible, or use a salad spinner. Remove the central stems only if they are large and tough – this is not necessary if you buy baby spinach leaves.

RICE & TOMATO SOUP

INGREDIENTS   Serves 4

150 g/5 oz easy-cook basmati
  rice
400 g can chopped tomatoes
2 garlic cloves, peeled and
  crushed
grated rind of ½ lime
2 tbsp extra-virgin olive oil
1 tsp sugar
salt and freshly ground pepper

300 ml/½ pint vegetable stock
  or water

FOR THE CROÛTONS:
2 tbsp prepared pesto sauce
2 tbsp olive oil
6 thin slices ciabatta bread, cut
  into 1 cm/½ inch cubes

1 Preheat the oven to 220°C/
425°F/Gas Mark 7. Rinse
and drain the basmati rice. Place
the canned tomatoes with their
juice in a large heavy-based
saucepan with the garlic, lime
rind, oil and sugar. Season to
taste with salt and pepper. Bring
to the boil, then reduce the heat,
cover and simmer for 10 minutes.

2 Add the boiling vegetable
stock or water and the rice,
then cook, uncovered, for a
further 15–20 minutes, or until
the rice is tender. If the soup
is too thick, add a little more
water. Reserve and keep warm,
if the croutons are not ready.

3 Meanwhile, to make the
croutons, mix the pesto and
olive oil in a large bowl. Add the
bread cubes and toss until they
are coated completely with the
mixture. Spread on a baking
sheet and bake in the preheated
oven for 10–15 minutes, until
golden and crisp, turning them

over halfway through cooking.
Serve the soup immediately
sprinkled with the warm croutons.

HELPFUL HINT

Pesto is a vivid green sauce,
made from basil leaves and
olive oil. Shop-bought pesto
is fine for this quick soup, but
try making your own during
the summer when basil is
plentiful. To make 150 ml/¼
pint of pesto, put 25 g/1 oz
fresh basil leaves (weighed
without stalks), 1 peeled garlic
clove, 1 tablespoon pine nuts,
4 tablespoons olive oil, salt
and black pepper in a blender
or food processor and blend
together at high speed until
very creamy. Stir in 25 g/1 oz
freshly grated Parmesan
cheese. Store in the refrigerator for up to 2 weeks in a
screw-topped jar .

COCONUT CHICKEN SOUP

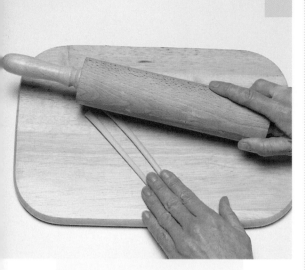

INGREDIENTS   Serves 4

2 lemon grass stalks

3 tbsp vegetable oil

3 medium onions, peeled and
  finely sliced

3 garlic cloves, peeled and
  crushed

2 tbsp fresh root ginger, finely
  grated

2–3 kaffir lime leaves

1½ tsp turmeric

1 red pepper, deseeded and
  diced

400 ml can coconut milk

1.1 litres/2 pints vegetable or
  chicken stock

275 g/9 oz easy-cook long-
  grain rice

275 g/10 oz cooked chicken
  meat

285 g can sweetcorn, drained

3 tbsp freshly chopped
  coriander

1 tbsp Thai fish sauce

freshly chopped pickled
  chillies, to serve

1 Discard the outer leaves of the lemon grass stalks, then place on a chopping board and, using a mallet or rolling pin, pound gently to bruise; reserve.

2 Heat the vegetable oil in a large saucepan and cook the onions over a medium heat for about 10–15 minutes until soft and beginning to change colour.

3 Lower the heat, stir in the garlic, ginger, lime leaves, turmeric and cook for 1 minute. Add the red pepper, coconut milk, stock, lemon grass and rice. Bring to the boil, cover and simmer gently over a low heat for about 10 minutes.

4 Cut the chicken into bite-sized pieces, then stir into the soup, with the sweetcorn and the freshly chopped coriander.

Add a few dashes of the Thai fish sauce to taste, then reheat gently, stirring frequently. Serve immediately with a few chopped pickled chillies to sprinkle on top.

FOOD FACT

Small dark glossy kaffir lime leaves come from a wild citrus tree and are usually imported from South-east Asia. They impart a strong and sharp, spicy citrus flavour and feature frequently in Thai and Indonesian soups. If you have difficulty finding them, substitute a large strip of lime or lemon rind instead, remembering to remove before serving.

HOT & SOUR MUSHROOM SOUP

INGREDIENTS   Serves 4

4 tbsp sunflower oil
3 garlic cloves, peeled and
  finely chopped
3 shallots, peeled and finely
  chopped
2 large red chillies, deseeded
  and finely chopped
1 tbsp soft brown sugar
large pinch of salt
1 litre/1¾ pints vegetable stock
250 g/9 oz Thai fragrant rice
5 kaffir lime leaves, torn
2 tbsp soy sauce

grated rind and juice of 1
  lemon
250 g/9 oz oyster mushrooms,
  wiped and cut into pieces
2 tbsp freshly chopped
  coriander

TO GARNISH:
2 green chillies, deseeded and
  finely chopped
3 spring onions, trimmed and
  finely chopped

1 Heat the oil in a frying pan, add the garlic and shallots and cook until golden brown and starting to crisp. Remove from the pan and reserve. Add the chillies to the pan and cook until they start to change colour.

2 Place the garlic, shallots and chillies in a food processor or blender and blend to a smooth purée with 150 ml /¼ pint water. Pour the purée back into the pan, add the sugar with a large pinch of salt, then cook gently, stirring, until dark in colour. Take care not to burn the mixture.

3 Pour the stock into a large saucepan, add the garlic purée, rice, lime leaves, soy sauce and the lemon rind and juice. Bring to the boil, then reduce the heat, cover and simmer gently for about 10 minutes.

4 Add the mushrooms and simmer for a further 10 minutes, or until the mushrooms and rice are tender. Remove the lime leaves, stir in the chopped coriander and ladle into bowls. Place the chopped green chillies and spring onions in small bowls and serve separately to sprinkle on top of the soup.

HELPFUL HINT

There are many kinds of chilli, varying in both size and colour, but they all have a hot, spicy flavour. They contain volatile oils which can irritate your skin, so during preparation take great care not to touch your eyes and wash your hands immediately after handling.

BACON & SPILT PEA SOUP

INGREDIENTS   Serves 4

50 g/2 oz dried split peas
25 g/1 oz butter
1 garlic clove, peeled and
  finely chopped
1 medium onion, peeled and
  thinly sliced
175 g/6 oz long-grain rice
2 tbsp tomato purée
1.1 litres/2 pints vegetable or
  chicken stock

175 g/6 oz carrots, peeled and
  finely diced
125 g/4 oz streaky bacon,
  finely chopped
salt and freshly ground black
  pepper
2 tbsp freshly chopped parsley
4 tbsp single cream
warm crusty garlic bread, to
  serve

1 Cover the dried split peas with plenty of cold water, cover loosely and leave to soak for a minimum of 12 hours, preferably overnight.

2 Melt the butter in a heavy-based saucepan, add the garlic and onion and cook for 2–3 minutes, without colouring. Add the rice, drained split peas and tomato purée and cook for 2–3 minutes, stirring constantly to prevent sticking. Add the stock, bring to the boil, then reduce the heat and simmer for 20–25 minutes, or until the rice and peas are tender. Remove from the heat and leave to cool.

3 Blend about three-quarters of the soup in a food processor or blender to form a smooth purée. Pour the purée into the remaining soup in the saucepan. Add the carrots to the saucepan and cook for a further 10–12 minutes, or until the carrots are tender.

4 Meanwhile, place the bacon in a non-stick frying pan and cook over a gentle heat until the bacon is crisp. Remove and drain on absorbent kitchen paper.

5 Season the soup with salt and pepper to taste, then stir in the parsley and cream. Reheat for 2–3 minutes, then ladle into soup bowls. Sprinkle with the bacon and serve immediately with warm garlic bread.

HELPFUL HINT

You can use either green or yellow split peas for this warming and satisfying soup – there is no difference in flavour. For a quicker alternative, use red split lentils as they are quick to cook and do not need pre-soaking.

PUMPKIN & SMOKED HADDOCK SOUP

INGREDIENTS   Serves 4–6

2 tbsp olive oil

1 medium onion, peeled and
  chopped

2 garlic cloves, peeled and
  chopped

3 celery stalks, trimmed and
  chopped

700 g/1½ lb pumpkin, peeled,
  deseeded and cut into
  chunks

450 g/1 lb potatoes, peeled
  and cut into chunks

750 ml/1¼ pints chicken stock,
  heated

125 ml/4 fl oz dry sherry

200 g/7 oz smoked haddock
  fillet

150 ml/¼ pint milk

freshly ground black pepper

2 tbsp freshly chopped parsley

1 Heat the oil in a large heavy-based saucepan and gently cook the onion, garlic, and celery for about 10 minutes. This will release the sweetness but not colour the vegetables. Add the pumpkin and potatoes to the saucepan and stir to coat the vegetables with the oil.

2 Gradually pour in the stock and bring to the boil. Cover, then reduce the heat and simmer for 25 minutes, stirring occasionally. Stir in the dry sherry, then remove the saucepan from the heat and leave to cool for 5–10 minutes.

3 Blend the mixture in a food processor or blender to form a chunky purée and return to the cleaned saucepan.

4 Meanwhile, place the fish in a shallow frying pan. Pour in the milk with 3 tablespoons of water and bring to almost boiling point. Reduce the heat, cover and simmer for 6 minutes, or until the fish is cooked and flakes easily. Remove from the heat and, using a slotted spoon remove the fish from the liquid, reserving both liquid and fish.

5 Discard the skin and any bones from the fish and flake into pieces. Stir the fish liquid into the soup, together with the flaked fish. Season with freshly ground black pepper, stir in the parsley and serve immediately.

TASTY TIP

Try to find undyed smoked haddock for this soup rather than the brightly coloured yellow type, as the texture and flavour is better.

COURGETTE & TARRAGON TORTILLA

INGREDIENTS
Serves 6

700 g/1½ lb potatoes
3 tbsp olive oil
1 onion, peeled and thinly sliced
salt and freshly ground black pepper

1 courgette, trimmed and thinly sliced
6 medium eggs
2 tbsp freshly chopped tarragon
tomato wedges, to serve

1 Peel the potatoes and thinly slice. Dry the slices in a clean tea towel to get them as dry as possible. Heat the oil in a large heavy-based pan, add the onion and cook for 3 minutes. Add the potatoes with a little salt and pepper, then stir the potatoes and onion lightly to coat in the oil.

2 Reduce the heat to the lowest possible setting, cover and cook gently for 5 minutes. Turn the potatoes and onion over and continue to cook for a further 5 minutes. Give the pan a shake every now and again to ensure that the potatoes do not stick to the base or burn. Add the courgette, then cover and cook for a further 10 minutes.

3 Beat the eggs and tarragon together and season to taste with salt and pepper. Pour the egg mixture over the vegetables and return to the heat. Cook on a low heat for up to 20–25 minutes, or until there is no liquid egg left on the surface of the tortilla.

4 Turn the tortilla over by inverting the tortilla onto the lid or onto a flat plate. Return the pan to the heat and cook for a final 3–5 minutes, or until the underside is golden brown. If preferred, place the tortilla under a preheated grill for 4 minutes, or until set and golden brown on top. Cut into small squares and serve hot or cold with tomato wedges.

FOOD FACT

Almost regarded as the national dish of Spain, this substantial omelette is traditionally made from eggs, potatoes and onions. Here, courgettes and tarragon are added for extra flavour and colour. Use even-sized waxy potatoes, which won't break up during cooking – *Maris Bard*, *Charlotte* or *Pentland Javelin* are all good choices of potato.

SMOKED SALMON SUSHI

INGREDIENTS   Serves 4

125 g/4 oz sushi rice or round
   pudding rice
2 tbsp cider vinegar
1 tbsp caster sugar
1 tsp salt
2 green leeks, trimmed

225 g/8 oz smoked salmon
1 tsp Japanese soy sauce

TO GARNISH:
few fresh chives
lemon or lime wedges

1 Wash the rice in plenty of cold water, then drain. Put the rice and 200 ml/7 fl oz cold water in a saucepan and leave to soak for 30 minutes. Place the saucepan over a medium heat and bring to the boil, stirring frequently. Lower the heat, cover and cook the rice for about 15 minutes, or until the grains are tender and the water has been absorbed. Remove from the heat and leave, still covered, for a further 10–15 minutes.

2 Place the vinegar, sugar and salt in a small saucepan. Heat gently, stirring to dissolve the sugar. Turn the rice into a large bowl, sprinkle over the vinegar mixture and mix through the rice.

3 Cut the trimmed leeks in half lengthways, then blanch in boiling water for 3–4 minutes. Drain and place in ice-cold water for 5 minutes, then drain.

4 Separate the leek leaves. Cut both the leek leaves and the salmon slices lengthways into 2.5 x 7.5 cm (1 x 3 inch) strips,

reserving 2 wide leek leaves. Place the leek slices neatly on top of the sliced salmon.

5 Spoon the rice onto the salmon and leek slices, then roll into parcels. Using the tip of a sharp knife, slice the reserved leek leaves lengthways into long strips. Tie the strips around the smoked salmon parcels. Sprinkle the parcels with a few drops of the soy sauce, garnish with the chives and lemon wedges and serve.

FOOD FACT

It takes many years of training to qualify as a sushi chef, but these smoked salmon and leek canapes are simple to make, although a little time consuming. Rolled sushi like these are known as Hosomaki in Japan. Use the rice straight away after cooking – it can not be stored in the refrigerator or it will harden and be difficult to work with.

POTATO PANCAKES

INGREDIENTS   Serves 6

FOR THE SAUCE:
4 tbsp crème fraîche
1 tbsp horseradish sauce
grated rind and juice of 1 lime
1 tbsp freshly snipped chives

225 g/8 oz floury potatoes,
   peeled and cut into chunks
1 small egg white
2 tbsp milk
2 tsp self-raising flour

1 tbsp freshly chopped thyme
large pinch of salt
a little vegetable oil, for frying
225 g/8 oz smoked mackerel
   fillets, skinned and roughly
   chopped
fresh herbs, to garnish

1 To make the sauce, mix together the crème fraîche, horseradish, lime rind and juice and chives. Cover and reserve.

2 Place the potatoes in a large saucepan and cover with lightly salted boiling water. Bring back to the boil, cover and simmer for 15 minutes, or until the potatoes are tender. Drain and mash until smooth. Cool for 5 minutes, then whisk in the egg white, milk, flour, thyme and salt to form a thick smooth batter. Leave to stand for 30 minutes, then stir before using.

3 Heat a little oil in a heavy-based frying pan. Add 2–3 large spoonfuls of batter to make a small pancake and cook for 1–2 minutes until golden. Flip the pancake and cook for a further minute, or until golden. Repeat with the remaining batter to make 8 pancakes.

4 Arrange the pancakes on a plate and top with the smoked mackerel. Garnish with herbs and serve immediately with spoonfuls of the reserved horseradish sauce.

HELPFUL HINT

Keep the pancakes warm as you make them by stacking on a warmed plate. Place greaseproof paper between each pancake to keep them separate and fold a clean tea towel loosely over the top. If preferred, the pancakes can be made in advance and frozen, interleaved with non-stick baking parchment. To serve, thaw, then reheat the stack of pancakes, covered in tinfoil, in a moderate oven.

SWEET POTATO CRISPS WITH MANGO SALSA

INGREDIENTS   Serves 6

FOR THE SALSA:
1 large mango, peeled, stoned
    and cut into small cubes
8 cherry tomatoes, quartered
½ cucumber, peeled if
    preferred and finely diced
1 red onion, peeled and finely
    chopped
pinch of sugar
1 red chilli, deseeded and
    finely chopped

2 tbsp rice vinegar
2 tbsp olive oil
grated rind and juice of 1 lime

450 g/1 lb sweet potatoes,
    peeled and thinly sliced
vegetable oil, for deep frying
sea salt
2 tbsp freshly chopped mint

1 To make the salsa, mix the mango with the tomatoes, cucumber and onion. Add the sugar, chilli, vinegar, oil and the lime rind and juice. Mix together thoroughly, cover and leave for 45–50 minutes.

2 Soak the potatoes in cold water for 40 minutes to remove as much of the excess starch as possible. Drain and dry thoroughly in a clean tea towel, or absorbent kitchen paper.

3 Heat the oil to 190°C/375°F in a deep fryer. When at the correct temperature, place half the potatoes in the frying basket, then carefully lower the potatoes into the hot oil and cook for 4–5 minutes, or until they are golden brown, shaking the basket every minute so that they do not stick together.

4 Drain the potato crisps on absorbent kitchen paper, sprinkle with sea salt and place under a preheated moderate grill for a few seconds to dry out. Repeat with the remaining potatoes. Stir the mint into the salsa and serve with the potato crisps.

HELPFUL HINT

Take care when deep-fat frying. Use a deep heavy-based saucepan or special deep-fat fryer and fill the pan no more than one-third with oil. If you do not have a food thermometer to check the temperature, drop a cube of bread into the oil. At the correct heat, it will turn golden brown in 40 seconds.

STUFFED VINE LEAVES

INGREDIENTS   Serves 6–8

150 g/5 oz long-grain rice
225 g/8 oz fresh or preserved
  vine leaves
225 g/8 oz red onion, peeled
  and finely chopped
3 baby leeks, trimmed and
  finely sliced
25 g/1 oz freshly chopped
  parsley
25 g/1 oz freshly chopped mint
25 g/1 oz freshly chopped dill
150 ml/¼ pint extra-virgin olive
  oil

salt and freshly ground black
  pepper
50 g/2 oz currants
50 g/2 oz ready-to-eat dried
  apricots, finely chopped
25 g/1 oz pine nuts
juice of 1 lemon
600–750 ml/1–1¼ pints boiling
  stock
lemon wedges or slices, to
  garnish
4 tbsp Greek-style yogurt, to
  serve

1 Soak the rice in cold water for 30 minutes. If using fresh vine leaves, blanch 5–6 leaves at a time, in salted boiling water for a minute. Rinse and drain. If using preserved vine leaves, soak in tepid water for at least 20 minutes, drain, rinse and pat dry with absorbent kitchen paper.

2 Mix the onion and leeks with the herbs and half the oil. Add the drained rice, mix and season to taste with salt and pepper. Stir in the currants, apricots, pine nuts and lemon juice. Spoon 1 teaspoon of the filling at the stalk end of each leaf. Roll, tucking the side flaps into the centre to create a neat parcel; do not roll too tight. Continue until all the filling is used.

3 Layer half the remaining vine leaves over the base of a large

frying pan. Pack the little parcels in the frying pan and cover with the remaining leaves.

4 Pour in enough stock to just cover the vine leaves, add a pinch of salt and bring to the boil. Reduce the heat, cover and simmer for 45–55 minutes, or until the rice is sticky and tender. Leave to stand for 10 minutes. Drain the stock. Garnish with lemon wedges and serve hot with the Greek yogurt.

FOOD FACT

The use of vine leaves in cooking goes back as far as the early cultivation of vines. Particularly popular in Middle Eastern cooking, they give a delicious, tart, grapey flavour to dishes.

POTATO SKINS

INGREDIENTS

Serves 4

4 large baking potatoes
2 tbsp olive oil
2 tsp paprika
125 g/4 oz pancetta, roughly chopped
6 tbsp double cream
125 g/4 oz Gorgonzola cheese
1 tbsp freshly chopped parsley

TO SERVE:
reduced-calorie mayonnaise
sweet chilli dipping sauce
tossed green salad

1 Preheat the oven to 200°C/ 400°F/Gas Mark 6. Scrub the potatoes, then prick a few times with a fork or skewer and place directly on the top shelf of the oven. Bake in the preheated oven for at least 1 hour, or until tender. The potatoes are cooked when they yield gently to the pressure of your hand.

2 Set the potatoes aside until cool enough to handle, then cut in half and scoop the flesh into a bowl and reserve. Preheat the grill and line the grill rack with tinfoil.

3 Mix together the oil and the paprika and use half to brush the outside of the potato skins. Place on the grill rack under the preheated hot grill and cook for 5 minutes, or until crisp, turning as necessary.

4 Heat the remaining paprika-flavoured oil and gently fry the pancetta until crisp. Add to the potato flesh along with the

cream, Gorgonzola cheese and parsley. Halve the potato skins and fill with the Gorgonzola filling. Return to the oven for a further 15 minutes to heat through. Sprinkle with a little more paprika and serve immediately with mayonnaise, sweet chilli sauce and a green salad.

FOOD FACT

A popular, well-known Italian cheese, Gorgonzola was first made over 1100 years ago in the village of the same name near Milan. Now mostly produced in Lombardy, it is made from pasteurised cows milk and allowed to ripen for at least 3 months, giving it a rich but not overpowering flavour. Unlike most blue cheeses, it should have a greater concentration of veining towards the centre of the cheese.

BEETROOT RISOTTO

INGREDIENTS
Serves 6

6 tbsp extra-virgin olive oil

1 onion, peeled and finely chopped

2 garlic cloves, peeled and finely chopped

2 tsp freshly chopped thyme

1 tsp grated lemon rind

350 g/12 oz Arborio rice

150 ml/¼ pint dry white wine

900 ml/1½ pints vegetable stock, heated

2 tbsp double cream

225 g/8 oz cooked beetroot, peeled and finely chopped

2 tbsp freshly chopped parsley

75 g/3 oz Parmesan cheese, freshly grated

salt and freshly ground black pepper

sprigs of fresh thyme, to garnish

1 Heat half the oil in a large heavy-based frying pan. Add the onion, garlic, thyme and lemon rind. Cook for 5 minutes, stirring frequently, until the onion is soft and transparent but not coloured. Add the rice and stir until it is well coated in the oil.

2 Add the wine, then bring to the boil and boil rapidly until the wine has almost evaporated. Reduce the heat.

3 Keeping the pan over a low heat, add a ladleful of the hot stock to the rice and cook, stirring constantly, until the stock is absorbed. Continue gradually adding the stock in this way until the rice is tender; this should take about 20 minutes. You may not need all the stock.

4 Stir in the cream, chopped beetroot, parsley and half the grated Parmesan cheese. Season to taste with salt and pepper. Garnish with sprigs of fresh thyme and serve immediately with the remaining grated Parmesan cheese.

TASTY TIP

If you buy ready-cooked beetroot, choose small ones, which are sweeter. Make sure that they are not doused in vinegar as this would spoil the flavour of the dish. If cooking your own, try baking them instead of boiling. Leave the stems intact and gently scrub to remove any dirt. Put them in a baking dish, cover loosely with tinfoil and cook in a preheated oven at 170°C/325°F/Gas Mark 3 for 2 hours. Once cool enough to handle, the skins should slip off.

GINGER & GARLIC POTATOES

INGREDIENTS — Serves 4

700 g/1½ lb potatoes
2.5 cm/1 inch piece of root ginger, peeled and coarsely chopped
3 garlic cloves, peeled and chopped
½ tsp turmeric
1 tsp salt
½ tsp cayenne pepper
5 tbsp vegetable oil
1 tsp whole fennel seeds

1 large eating apple, cored and diced
6 spring onions, trimmed and sliced diagonally
1 tbsp freshly chopped coriander

TO SERVE:
assorted bitter salad leaves
curry-flavoured mayonnaise

1 Scrub the potatoes, then place, unpeeled, in a large saucepan and cover with boiling salted water. Bring to the boil and cook for 15 minutes, then drain and leave the potatoes to cool completely. Peel and cut into 2.5 cm/1 inch cubes.

2 Place the root ginger, garlic, turmeric, salt and cayenne pepper in a food processor and blend for 1 minute. With the motor still running, slowly add 3 tablespoons of water and blend into a paste. Alternatively, pound the ingredients to a paste with a pestle and mortar.

3 Heat the oil in a large heavy-based frying pan and when hot, but not smoking, add the fennel seeds and fry for a few minutes. Stir in the ginger paste and cook for 2 minutes, stirring frequently. Take care not to burn the mixture.

4 Reduce the heat, then add the potatoes and cook for 5–7 minutes, stirring frequently, until the potatoes have a golden-brown crust. Add the diced apple and spring onions, then sprinkle with the freshly chopped coriander. Heat through for 2 minutes, then serve on assorted salad leaves with curry-flavoured mayonnaise.

FOOD FACT

Turmeric is a rhizome that comes from the same family as ginger. When the root is dried, it has a dull yellow appearance and can be ground to a powder. Turmeric powder can be used in a wide range of savoury dishes. It has a warm spicy flavour, and gives food a wonderful golden colour.

THAI CRAB CAKES

INGREDIENTS

Serves 4

200 g/7 oz easy-cook basmati rice

450 ml/¾ pint chicken stock, heated

200 g/7 oz cooked crab meat

125 g/ 4 oz cod fillet, skinned and minced

5 spring onions, trimmed and finely chopped

1 lemon grass stalk, outer leaves discarded and finely chopped

1 green chilli, deseeded and finely chopped

1 tbsp freshly grated root ginger

1 tbsp freshly chopped coriander

1 tbsp plain flour

1 medium egg

salt and freshly ground black pepper

2 tbsp vegetable oil, for frying

TO SERVE:

sweet chilli dipping sauce

fresh salad leaves

1 Put the rice in a large saucepan and add the hot stock. Bring to the boil, cover and simmer over a low heat, without stirring, for 18 minutes, or until the grains are tender and all the liquid is absorbed.

2 To make the cakes, place the crab meat, fish, spring onions, lemon grass, chilli, ginger, coriander, flour and egg in a food processor. Blend until all the ingredients are mixed thoroughly, then season to taste with salt and pepper. Add the rice to the processor and blend once more, but do not over mix.

3 Remove the mixture from the processor and place on a clean work surface. With damp hands, divide into 12 even-sized patties. Transfer to a plate, cover and chill in the refrigerator for about 30 minutes.

4 Heat the oil in a heavy-based frying pan and cook the crab cakes, 4 at a time, for 3–5 minutes on each side until crisp and golden. Drain on absorbent kitchen paper and serve immediately with a chilli dipping sauce.

HELPFUL HINT

For the best flavour and texture use fresh cooked crab for this dish, choosing the white rather than brown meat. Canned crab meat will still give good results. Simply drain in a sieve and rinse very briefly under cold water to remove the excess brine before using.

RICE & PAPAYA SALAD

INGREDIENTS   Serves 4

175 g/6 oz easy-cook basmati
  rice
1 cinnamon stick, bruised
1 bird's-eye chilli, deseeded
  and finely chopped
rind and juice of 2 limes
rind and juice of 2 lemons
2 tbsp Thai fish sauce
1 tbsp soft light brown sugar
1 papaya, peeled and seeds
  removed

1 mango, peeled and stone
  removed
1 green chilli, deseeded and
  finely chopped
2 tbsp freshly chopped
  coriander
1 tbsp freshly chopped mint
250 g/9 oz cooked chicken
50 g/2 oz roasted peanuts,
  chopped
strips of pitta bread, to serve

1 Rinse and drain the rice and pour into a saucepan. Add 450 ml/¾ pint boiling salted water and the cinnamon stick. Bring to the boil, reduce the heat to a very low heat, cover and cook without stirring for 15–18 minutes, or until all the liquid is absorbed. The rice should be light and fluffy and have steam holes on the surface. Remove the cinnamon stick and stir in the rind from 1 lime.

2 To make the dressing, place the bird's-eye chilli, remaining rind and lime and lemon juice, fish sauce and sugar in a food processor, mix for a few minutes until blended. Alternatively, place all these ingredients in a screw-top jar and shake until well blended. Pour half the dressing over the hot rice and toss until the rice glistens.

3 Slice the papaya and mango into thin slices, then place in a bowl. Add the chopped green chilli, coriander and mint. Place the chicken on a chopping board, then remove and discard any skin or sinews. Cut into fine shreds and add to the bowl with the chopped peanuts.

4 Add the remaining dressing to the chicken mixture and stir until all the ingredients are lightly coated. Spoon the rice onto a platter, pile the chicken mixture on top and serve with warm strips of pitta bread.

HELPFUL HINT

The papaya or pawpaw's skin turns from green when unripe, through to yellow and orange. To prepare, cut in half lengthways, scoop out the black seeds with a teaspoon and discard. Cut away the thin skin before slicing.

TRADITIONAL FISH PIE

INGREDIENTS
Serves 4

450 g/1 lb cod or coley fillets, skinned

450 ml/¾ pint milk

1 small onion, peeled and quartered

salt and freshly ground black pepper

900 g/2 lb potatoes, peeled and cut into chunks

100 g/3½ oz butter

125 g/4 oz large prawns

2 large eggs, hard-boiled and quartered

198 g can sweetcorn, drained

2 tbsp freshly chopped parsley

3 tbsp plain flour

50 g/2 oz Cheddar cheese, grated

1 Preheat the oven to 200°C/ 400°F/Gas Mark 6, about 15 minutes before cooking. Place the fish in a shallow frying pan, pour over 300 ml/½ pint of the milk and add the onion. Season to taste with salt and pepper. Bring to the boil and simmer for 8–10 minutes until the fish is cooked. Remove the fish with a slotted spoon and place in a 1.4 litre/ 2½ pint baking dish. Strain the cooking liquid and reserve.

2 Boil the potatoes until soft, then mash with 40 g/1½ oz of the butter and 2–3 tablespoons of the remaining milk. Reserve.

3 Arrange the prawns and sliced eggs on top of the fish, then scatter over the sweetcorn and sprinkle with the parsley.

4 Melt the remaining butter in a saucepan, stir in the flour and cook gently for 1 minute, stirring. Whisk in the reserved cooking liquid and remaining milk. Cook for 2 minutes, or until thickened, then pour over the fish mixture and cool slightly.

5 Spread the mashed potato over the top of the pie and sprinkle over the grated cheese. Bake in the preheated over for 30 minutes until golden. Serve immediately.

TASTY TIP

Any variety of white fish may be used in this delicious dish, including haddock, hake, ling, pollack and whiting. You could also used smoked fish, such as smoked cod or haddock for a change. After simmering in milk, carefully check and remove any bones from the cooked fish.

SEAFOOD RISOTTO

INGREDIENTS
Serves 4

50 g/2 oz butter
2 shallots, peeled and finely
  chopped
1 garlic clove, peeled and
  crushed
350 g/12 oz Arborio rice
150 ml/¼ pint white wine
600 ml/1 pint fish or vegetable
  stock, heated

125 g/4 oz large peel prawns
290 g can baby clams
50 g/2 oz smoked salmon
  trimmings
2 tbsp freshly chopped parsley

TO SERVE:
green salad
crusty bread

1 Melt the butter in a large, heavy-based saucepan, add the shallots and garlic and cook for 2 minutes until slightly softened. Add the rice and cook for 1–2 minutes, stirring continuously, then pour in the wine and boil for 1 minute.

2 Pour in half the hot stock, bring to the boil, cover the saucepan and simmer gently for 15 minutes, adding the remaining stock a little at a time. Continue to simmer for 5 minutes, or until the rice is cooked and all the liquid is absorbed.

3 Meanwhile, prepare the fish by peeling the prawns and removing the heads and tails. Drain the clams and discard the liquid. Cut the smoked salmon trimmings into thin strips.

4 When the rice has cooked, stir in the prawns, clams, smoked salmon strips and half the chopped parsley, then heat

through for 1–2 minutes until everything is piping hot. Turn into a serving dish, sprinkle with the remaining parsley and the Parmesan cheese and serve immediately with a green salad and crusty bread.

TASTY TIP

A good-quality stock will make a huge difference to the finished flavour of this risotto. Rinse 900 g/2 lb fish bones and trimmings and put in a large saucepan with 1 carrot, 1 onion and 1 celery stalk, all peeled and roughly chopped, 1 bouquet garni, 4 pepper-corns and 900 ml/1½ pints cold water. Slowly bring to the boil, then skim. Cover and simmer for 30 minutes. Strain the stock through a fine sieve, cool and chill in the refrigerator for up to 2 days. After chilling, boil vigorously before using.

SMOKED HADDOCK KEDGEREE

INGREDIENTS Serves 4

450 g/1 lb smoked haddock fillets

50 g/2 oz butter

1 onion, peeled and finely chopped

2 tsp mild curry powder

175 g/6 oz long-grain rice

450 ml/¾ pint fish or vegetable stock, heated

2 large eggs, hard-boiled and shelled

2 tbsp freshly chopped parsley

2 tbsp whipping cream (optional)

salt and freshly ground black pepper

pinch of cayenne pepper

1 Place the haddock in a shallow frying pan and cover with 300 ml/½ pint water. Simmer gently for 8–10 minutes, or until the fish is cooked. Drain, then remove all the skin and bones from the fish and flake into a dish. Keep warm.

2 Melt the butter in a saucepan and add the chopped onion and curry powder. Cook, stirring, for 3–4 minutes, or until the onion is soft, then stir in the rice. Cook for a further minute, stirring continuously, then stir in the hot stock.

3 Cover and simmer gently for 15 minutes, or until the rice has absorbed all the liquid. Cut the eggs into quarters or eighths and add half to the mixture with half the parsley.

4 Carefully fold in the cooked fish to the mixture and add the cream, if using. Season to taste with salt and pepper.

Heat the kedgeree through briefly until piping hot.

5 Transfer the mixture to a large dish and garnish with the remaining quartered eggs, parsley and serve with a pinch of cayenne pepper. Serve immediately.

FOOD FACT

The word *Khichri* means a mixture or hotchpotch in Hindi. The British in India adapted this dish, which was originally made with an assortment of spices simmered with rice and lentils, and turned it into kedgeree, adding flakes of smoked fish and hard-boiled eggs.

TUNA FISH BURGERS

INGREDIENTS   Makes 8

450 g/1 lb potatoes, peeled
  and cut into chunks
50 g/2 oz butter
2 tbsp milk
400 g can tuna in oil
1 spring onion, trimmed and
  finely chopped
1 tbsp freshly chopped parsley
salt and freshly ground black
  pepper
2 medium eggs, beaten

2 tbsp seasoned plain flour
125 g/4 oz fresh white
  breadcrumbs
4 tbsp vegetable oil
4 sesame seed baps (optional)

TO SERVE:
fat chips
mixed salad
tomato chutney

1 Place the potatoes in a large saucepan, cover with boiling water and simmer until soft. Drain, then mash with 40 g/1½ oz of the butter and the milk. Turn into a large bowl. Drain the tuna, discarding the oil and flake into the bowl of potato. Stir well to mix.

2 Add the spring onions and parsley to the mixture and season to taste with salt and pepper. Add 1 tablespoon of the beaten egg to bind the mixture together. Chill in the refrigerator for at least 1 hour.

3 Shape the chilled mixture with your hands into 4 large burgers. First, coat the burgers with seasoned flour, then brush them with the remaining beaten egg, allowing any excess to drip back into the bowl. Finally, coat them evenly in the breadcrumbs, pressing the crumbs on with your hands, if necessary.

4 Heat a little of the oil in a frying pan and fry the burgers for 2–3 minutes on each side until golden, adding more oil if necessary. Drain on absorbent kitchen paper and serve hot in baps, if using, with chips, mixed salad and chutney.

HELPFUL HINT

Drain the potatoes thoroughly and dry them over a very low heat before mashing with the milk and butter to ensure the mixture isn't too soft to shape. If time allows, cover the bread-coated burgers with clingfilm and chill in the refrigerator for 30 minutes before cooking so that they are really firm.

SALMON FISH CAKES

INGREDIENTS   Serves 4

450 g/1 lb salmon fillet,
    skinned
salt and freshly ground black
    pepper
450 g/1 lb potatoes, peeled
    and cut into chunks
25 g/1 oz butter
1 tbsp milk
2 medium tomatoes, skinned,
    deseeded and chopped
2 tbsp freshly chopped parsley

75 g/3 oz wholemeal
    breadcrumbs
25 g/1 oz Cheddar cheese,
    grated
2 tbsp plain flour
2 medium eggs, beaten
3–4 tbsp vegetable oil

TO SERVE:
ready-made raita
sprigs of fresh mint

1 Place the salmon in a shallow frying pan and cover with water. Season to taste with salt and pepper and simmer for 8–10 minutes until the fish is cooked. Drain and flake into a bowl.

2 Boil the potatoes in lightly salted water until soft, then drain. Mash with the butter and milk until smooth. Add the potato to the bowl of fish and stir in the tomatoes and half the parsley. Adjust the seasoning to taste. Chill the mixture in the refrigerator for at least 2 hours to firm up.

3 Mix the breadcrumbs with the grated cheese and the remaining parsley. When the fish mixture is firm, form into 8 flat cakes. First, lightly coat the fish cakes in the flour, then dip into the beaten egg, allowing any excess to drip back into the bowl. Finally, press into the breadcrumb mixture until well coated.

4 Heat a little of the oil in a frying pan and fry the fish cakes in batches for 2–3 minutes on each side until golden and crisp, adding more oil if necessary. Serve with raita garnished with sprigs of mint.

HELPFUL HINT

To remove the skins from the tomatoes, pierce each with the tip of a sharp knife, then plunge into boiling water and leave for up to 1 minute. Drain, then rinse in cold water – the skins should peel off easily. Alternatively, hold them over a gas flame with a fork for a few seconds, turning until the skin is slightly blackened and blistered.

BATTERED COD & CHUNKY CHIPS

INGREDIENTS

Serves 4

15 g/½ oz fresh yeast
300 ml/½ pint beer
225 g/8 oz plain flour
1 tsp salt
700 g/1½ lb potatoes
450 ml/¾ pint groundnut oil
4 cod fillets, about 225 g/8 oz
    each, skinned and boned
2 tbsp seasoned plain flour

TO GARNISH:
lemon wedges
sprigs of flat-leaf parsley

TO SERVE:
tomato ketchup
vinegar

1 Dissolve the yeast with a little of the beer in a jug and mix to a paste. Pour in the remaining beer, whisking all the time until smooth. Place the flour and salt in a bowl, and gradually pour in the beer mixture, whisking continuously to make a thick smooth batter. Cover the bowl and allow the batter to stand at room temperature for 1 hour.

2 Peel the potatoes and cut into thick slices. Cut each slice lengthways to make chunky chips. Place them in a non-stick frying pan and heat, shaking the pan until all the moisture has evaporated. Turn them onto absorbent kitchen paper to dry off.

3 Heat the oil to 180°C/350°F, then fry the chips a few at a time for 4–5 minutes until crisp and golden. Drain on absorbent kitchen paper and keep warm.

4 Pat the cod fillets dry, then coat in the flour. Dip the floured fillets into the reserved batter. Fry for 2–3 minutes until cooked and crisp, then drain. Garnish with lemon wedges and parsley and serve immediately with the chips, tomato ketchup and vinegar.

HELPFUL HINT

When mixed with warm liquid, yeast produces gases which lighten this batter. Fresh yeast can be bought in health food shops, large supermarkets with in-store bakeries, and some bakers. Check that it is moist and creamy-coloured and has a strong yeasty smell. If it is dry, discoloured and crumbly, it is probably stale and will not work well. Store fresh yeast well-wrapped in the refrigerator for up to 3 days. Alternatively, it can be frozen, but should be used within 3 months.

PAELLA

INGREDIENTS   Serves 6

450 g/1 lb live mussels
4 tbsp olive oil
6 medium chicken thighs
1 medium onion, peeled and
  finely chopped
1 garlic clove, peeled and
  crushed
225 g/8 oz tomatoes, skinned,
  deseeded and chopped
1 red pepper, deseeded and
  chopped
1 green pepper, deseeded and
  chopped
125 g/4 oz frozen peas

1 tsp paprika
450 g/1 lb Arborio rice
½ tsp turmeric
900 ml/1½ pints chicken stock,
  warmed
175 g/6 oz large peeled
  prawns
salt and freshly ground black
  pepper
2 limes
1 lemon
1 tbsp freshly chopped basil
whole cooked unpeeled
  prawns, to garnish

1 Rinse the mussels under cold running water, scrubbing well to remove any grit and barnacles, then pull off the hairy 'beards'. Tap any open mussels sharply with a knife, and discard if they refuse to close.

2 Heat the oil in a paella pan or large, heavy-based frying pan and cook the chicken thighs for 10–15 minutes until golden. Remove and keep warm.

3 Fry the onion and garlic in the remaining oil in the pan for 2–3 minutes, then add the tomatoes, peppers, peas and paprika and cook for a further 3 minutes.

4 Add the rice to the pan and return the chicken with the turmeric and half the stock.

Bring to the boil and simmer, gradually adding more stock as it is absorbed. Cook for 20 minutes, or until most of the stock has been absorbed and the rice is almost tender.

5 Put the mussels in a large saucepan with 5 cm/2 inches boiling salted water, cover and steam for 5 minutes. Discard any with shells that have not opened, then stir into the rice with the prawns. Season to taste with salt and pepper. Heat through for 2–3 minutes until piping hot. Squeeze the juice from 1 of the limes over the paella.

6 Cut the remaining limes and the lemon into wedges and arrange on top of the paella. Sprinkle with the basil, garnish with the prawns and serve.

RUSSIAN FISH PIE

INGREDIENTS   Serves 4–6

450 g/1 lb orange roughly or
  haddock fillet
150 ml/¼ pint dry white wine
salt and freshly ground black
  pepper
75 g/3 oz butter or margarine
1 large onion, peeled and
  finely chopped
75 g/3 oz long-grain rice
1 tbsp freshly chopped dill
125 g/4 oz baby button
  mushrooms, quartered

125 g/4 oz peeled prawns,
  thawed if frozen
3 medium eggs, hard-boiled
  and chopped
550 g/1¼ lb ready-prepared
  puff pastry, thawed if frozen
1 small egg, beaten with a
  pinch of salt
assorted bitter salad leaves,
  to serve

1 Preheat the oven to 200°C/
400°F/Gas Mark 6, 15
minutes before cooking. Place the
fish in a shallow frying pan with
the wine, 150 ml/¼ pint water and
salt and pepper. Simmer for 8–10
minutes. Strain the fish, reserving
the liquid, and when cool enough
to handle, flake into a bowl.

2 Melt the butter or margarine
in a saucepan and cook the
onions for 2–3 minutes, then add
the rice, reserved fish liquid and
dill. Season lightly. Cover and
simmer for 10 minutes, then stir
in the mushrooms and cook for a
further 10 minutes, or until all
the liquid is absorbed. Mix the
rice with the cooked fish, prawns
and eggs. Leave to cool.

3 Roll half the pastry out
on a lightly floured surface
into a 23 x 30.5 cm/9 x 12 inch
rectangle. Place on a dampened

baking sheet and arrange the fish
mixture on top, leaving a 1 cm/
½ inch border. Brush the border
with a little water.

4 Roll out the remaining pastry
to a rectangle and use to
cover the fish. Brush the edges
lightly with a little of the beaten
egg and press to seal. Roll out
the pastry trimmings and use
to decorate the top. Chill in the
refrigerator for 30 minutes. Brush
with the beaten egg and bake for
30 minutes, or until golden. Serve
immediately with salad leaves.

FOOD FACT

Kulebyaka or Koulubiac is a
classic festive dish from
Russia. It is traditionally made
with a yeasted dough, but
ready-made puff pastry works
well as an easy alternative.

Tuna & Mushroom Ragout

INGREDIENTS   Serves 4

225 g/8 oz basmati and wild
  rice
50 g/2 oz butter
1 tbsp olive oil
1 large onion, peeled and
  finely chopped
1 garlic clove, peeled and
  crushed
300 g/11 oz baby button
  mushrooms, wiped and
  halved
2 tbsp plain flour
400 g can chopped tomatoes

1 tbsp freshly chopped parsley
dash of Worcestershire sauce
400 g can tuna in oil, drained
salt and freshly ground black
  pepper
4 tbsp Parmesan cheese,
  grated
1 tbsp freshly shredded basil

TO SERVE:
green salad
garlic bread

1 Cook the basmati and wild
rice in a saucepan of boiling
salted water for 20 minutes, then
drain and return to the pan. Stir
in half of the butter, cover the
pan and leave to stand for 2
minutes until all of the butter
has melted.

2 Heat the oil and the
remaining butter in a frying
pan and cook the onion for 1–2
minutes until soft. Add the
garlic and mushrooms and
continue to cook for a further
3 minutes.

3 Stir in the flour and cook
for 1 minute, then add the
tomatoes and bring the sauce
to the boil. Add the parsley,
Worcestershire sauce and tuna
and simmer gently for 3 minutes.
Season to taste with salt and
freshly ground pepper.

4 Stir the rice well, then spoon
onto 4 serving plates and top
with the tuna and mushroom
mixture. Sprinkle with a spoonful
of grated Parmesan cheese and
some shredded basil for each
portion and serve immediately
with a green salad and chunks of
garlic bread.

TASTY TIP

Fresh basil adds a wonderful
flavour and fragrance to this
dish, but sometimes it can be
difficult to find during the
winter months. If you have
problems finding it, buy
chopped tomatoes that have
basil already added to them,
or use extra freshly chopped
parsley instead.

COCONUT FISH CURRY

INGREDIENTS

Serves 4

2 tbsp sunflower oil

1 medium onion, peeled and
very finely chopped

1 yellow pepper, deseeded
and finely chopped

1 garlic clove, peeled and
crushed

1 tbsp mild curry paste

2.5 cm/1 inch piece of root
ginger, peeled and grated

1 red chilli, deseeded and
finely chopped

400 ml can coconut milk

700 g/1½ lb firm white fish,
e.g. monkfish fillets, skinned
and cut into chunks

225 g/8 oz basmati rice

1 tbsp freshly chopped
coriander

1 tbsp mango chutney

salt and freshly ground black
pepper

TO GARNISH:

lime wedges

fresh coriander sprigs

TO SERVE:

Greek yogurt

warm naan bread

1 Put 1 tablespoon of the oil into a large frying pan and cook the onion, pepper and garlic for 5 minutes, or until soft. Add the remaining oil, curry paste, ginger and chilli and cook for a further minute.

2 Pour in the coconut milk and bring to the boil, reduce the heat and simmer gently for 5 minutes, stirring occasionally. Add the monkfish to the pan and continue to simmer gently for 5–10 minutes, or until the fish is tender, but not overcooked.

3 Meanwhile, cook the rice in a saucepan of boiling salted water for 15 minutes, or until tender. Drain the rice thoroughly and turn out into a serving dish.

4 Stir the chopped coriander and chutney gently into the fish curry and season to taste with salt and pepper. Spoon the fish curry over the cooked rice, garnish with lime wedges and coriander sprigs and serve immediately with spoonfuls of Greek yogurt and warm naan bread.

FOOD FACT

Coconut milk is the liquid extracted from grated and pressed coconut flesh, combined with a little water.

CHUNKY HALIBUT CASSEROLE

INGREDIENTS   Serves 6

50 g/2 oz butter or margarine
2 large onions, peeled and
   sliced into rings
1 red pepper, deseeded and
   roughly chopped
450 g/1 lb potatoes, peeled
450 g/1 lb courgettes, trimmed
   and thickly sliced
2 tbsp plain flour
1 tbsp paprika
2 tsp vegetable oil

300 ml/½ pint white wine
150 ml/¼ pint fish stock
400 g can chopped tomatoes
2 tbsp freshly chopped basil
salt and freshly ground black
   pepper
450 g/1 lb halibut fillet,
   skinned and cut into 2.5 cm/
   1 inch cubes
sprigs of fresh basil, to garnish
freshly cooked rice, to serve

1 Melt the butter or margarine in a large saucepan, add the onions and pepper and cook for 5 minutes, or until softened.

2 Cut the peeled potatoes into 2.5 cm/1 inch dice, rinse lightly and shake dry, then add them to the onions and pepper in the saucepan. Add the courgettes and cook, stirring frequently, for a further 2–3 minutes.

3 Sprinkle the flour, paprika and vegetable oil into the saucepan and cook, stirring continuously, for 1 minute. Pour in 150 ml/¼ pint of the wine, with all the stock and the chopped tomatoes, and bring to the boil.

4 Add the basil to the casserole, season to taste with salt and pepper and cover. Simmer for 15 minutes, then add the halibut and the remaining wine and

simmer very gently for a further 5–7 minutes, or until the fish and vegetables are just tender. Garnish with basil sprigs and serve immediately with freshly cooked rice.

FOOD FACT

Halibut is a flatfish with firm, milky white flesh that has an almost meaty texture, making it ideal for this casserole. They can grow to an enormous size, at times weighing in at over 200 kg/ 444 lb, and are fished in the deep, freezing-cold waters of the North Sea.

MEDITERRANEAN CHOWDER

INGREDIENTS   Serves 6

1 tbsp olive oil

1 tbsp butter

1 large onion, peeled and
finely sliced

4 celery stalks, trimmed and
thinly sliced

2 garlic cloves, peeled and
crushed

1 bird's-eye chilli, deseeded
and finely chopped

1 tbsp plain flour

225 g/8 oz potatoes, peeled
and diced

600 ml/1 pint fish or vegetable
stock

700 g/1½ lb whiting or cod fillet
cut into 2.5 cm/1 inch cubes

2 tbsp freshly chopped parsley

125 g/4 oz large peeled
prawns

198 g can sweetcorn, drained

salt and freshly ground black
pepper

150 ml/¼ pint single cream

1 tbsp freshly snipped chives

warm, crusty bread, to serve

1 Heat the oil and butter together in a large saucepan, add the onion, celery and garlic and cook gently for 2–3 minutes until softened. Add the chilli and stir in the flour. Cook, stirring, for a further minute.

2 Add the potatoes to the saucepan with the stock. Bring to the boil, cover and simmer for 10 minutes. Add the fish cubes to the saucepan with the chopped parsley and cook for a further 5–10 minutes, or until the fish and potatoes are just tender.

3 Stir in the peeled prawns and sweetcorn and season to taste with salt and pepper. Pour in the cream and adjust the seasoning, if necessary.

4 Scatter the snipped chives over the top of the chowder.

Ladle into 6 large bowls and serve immediately with plenty of warm crusty bread.

FOOD FACT

A chowder is a classic meal-in-a-bowl soup whose name originates from the French *chaudiere* (the pot used by settlers in the southern states of America for making soups and stews). Chowders are usually fish based and often feature sweetcorn. This version has been thickened with potatoes.

SPANISH OMELETTE WITH SMOKED COD

INGREDIENTS   Serves 3–4

3 tbsp sunflower oil

350 g/12 oz potatoes, peeled and cut into 1 cm/½ inch cubes

2 medium onions, peeled and cut into wedges

2–4 large garlic cloves, peeled and thinly sliced

1 large red pepper, deseeded, quartered and thinly sliced

125 g/4 oz smoked cod

salt and freshly ground black pepper

25 g/1 oz butter, melted

1 tbsp double cream

6 medium eggs, beaten

2 tbsp freshly chopped flat-leaf parsley

50 g/2 oz mature Cheddar cheese, grated

TO SERVE:

crusty bread

tossed green salad, to serve

1 Heat the oil in a large non-stick heavy-based frying pan, add the potatoes, onions and garlic and cook gently for 10–15 minutes until golden brown, then add the red pepper and cook for 3 minutes.

2 Meanwhile, place the fish in a shallow frying pan and cover with water. Season to taste with salt and pepper and poach gently for 10 minutes. Drain and flake the fish into a bowl, toss in the melted butter and cream, adjust the seasoning and reserve.

3 When the vegetables are cooked, drain off any excess oil and stir in the beaten egg with the chopped parsley. Pour the fish mixture over the top and cook

gently for 5 minutes, or until the eggs become firm.

4 Sprinkle the grated cheese over the top and place the pan under a preheated hot grill. Cook for 2–3 minutes until the cheese is golden and bubbling. Carefully slide the omelette onto a large plate and serve immediately with plenty of bread and salad.

HELPFUL HINT

For best results, Spanish omelette should be cooked slowly until set. Finishing the dish under the grill gives it a delicious golden look.

SUPREME BAKED POTATOES

INGREDIENTS   Serves 4

4 large baking potatoes
40 g/1½ oz butter
1 tbsp sunflower oil
1 carrot, peeled and chopped
2 celery stalks, trimmed and
   finely chopped
200 g can white crab meat

2 spring onions, trimmed and
   finely chopped
salt and freshly ground black
   pepper
50 g/2 oz Cheddar cheese,
   grated
tomato salad, to serve

1 Preheat the oven to 200°C/ 400°F/Gas Mark 6. Scrub the potatoes and prick all over with a fork, or thread 2 potatoes onto 2 long metal skewers. Place the potatoes in the preheated oven for 1–1½ hours, or until soft to the touch. Allow to cool a little, then cut in half.

2 Scoop out the cooked potato and turn into a bowl, leaving a reasonably firm potato shell. Mash the cooked potato flesh, then mix in the butter and mash until the butter has melted.

3 While the potatoes are cooking, heat the oil in a frying pan and cook the carrot and celery for 2 minutes. Cover the pan tightly and continue to cook for another 5 minutes, or until the vegetables are tender.

4 Add the cooked vegetables to the bowl of mashed potato and mix well. Fold in the crab meat and the spring onions, then season to taste with salt and pepper.

5 Pile the mixture back into the potato shells and press in firmly. Sprinkle the grated cheese over the top and return the potato halves to the oven for 12–15 minutes until hot, golden and bubbling. Serve immediately with a tomato salad.

TASTY TIP

Threading the potatoes onto metal skewers helps them to cook more evenly and quickly as heat is transferred via the metal to the centres of the potatoes during cooking. To give the skins a crunchier finish, rub them with a little oil and lightly sprinkle with salt before baking.

SMOKED SALMON QUICHE

INGREDIENTS
Serves 6

225 g/8 oz plain flour
50 g/2 oz butter
50 g/2 oz white vegetable fat
  or lard
2 tsp sunflower oil
225 g/8 oz potato, peeled and
  diced
125 g/4 oz Gruyère cheese,
  grated
75 g/3 oz smoked salmon
  trimmings

5 medium eggs, beaten
300 ml/½ pint single cream
salt and freshly ground black
  pepper
1 tbsp freshly chopped flat-
  leaf parsley

TO SERVE:
mixed salad
baby new potatoes

1 Preheat the oven to 200°C/ 400°F/Gas Mark 6. Blend the flour, butter and white vegetable fat or lard together until it resembles fine breadcrumbs. Blend again, adding sufficient water to make a firm but pliable dough. Use the dough to line a 23 cm/9 inch flan dish or tin, then chill the pastry case in the refrigerator for 30 minutes. Bake blind with baking beans for 10 minutes.

2 Heat the oil in a small frying pan, add the diced potato and cook for 3–4 minutes until lightly browned. Reduce the heat and cook for 2–3 minutes, or until tender. Leave to cool.

3 Scatter the grated cheese evenly over the base of the pastry case, then arrange the cooled potato on top. Add the smoked salmon in an even layer.

4 Beat the eggs with the cream and season to taste with salt and pepper. Whisk in the parsley and pour the mixture carefully into the dish.

5 Reduce the oven to 180°C/ 350°F/Gas Mark 4 and bake for about 30–40 minutes, or until the filling is set and golden. Serve hot or cold with a mixed salad and baby new potatoes.

TASTY TIP

Using lard or white vegetable fat with the butter makes a deliciously short-textured pastry, but you can use all butter if you prefer a richer flavour and colour. Do not be tempted to leave out the chilling time for the pastry case. This allows the pastry to rest and helps to minimise shrinkage during baking.

SMOKED MACKEREL & POTATO SALAD

INGREDIENTS   Serves 4

½ tsp dry mustard powder
1 large egg yolk
salt and freshly ground black
   pepper
150 ml/¼ pint sunflower oil
1–2 tbsp lemon juice
450 g/1 lb baby new potatoes
25 g/1 oz butter
350 g/12 oz smoked mackerel
   fillets

4 celery stalks, trimmed and
   finely chopped
3 tbsp creamed horseradish
150 ml/¼ pint crème fraîche
1 Little Gem, rinsed and
   roughly torn
8 cherry tomatoes, halved

1 Place the mustard powder and egg yolk in a small bowl with salt and pepper and whisk until blended. Add the oil, drop by drop, into the egg mixture, whisking continuously. When the mayonnaise is thick, add the lemon juice, drop by drop, until a smooth, glossy consistency is formed. Reserve.

2 Cook the potatoes in boiling salted water until tender, then drain. Cool slightly, then cut into halves or quarters, depending on size. Return to the saucepan and toss in the butter.

3 Remove the skin from the mackerel fillets and flake into pieces. Add to the potatoes in the saucepan, together with the celery.

4 Blend 4 tablespoons of the mayonnaise with the horseradish and crème fraîche. Season to taste with salt and pepper, then add to the potato and mackerel mixture and stir lightly.

5 Arrange the lettuce and tomatoes on 4 serving plates. Pile the smoked mackerel mixture on top of the lettuce, grind over a little pepper and serve with the remaining mayonnaise.

HELPFUL HINT

When making mayonnaise, ensure that the ingredients are at room temperature, or it may curdle. For speed, it can be made in a food processor: briefly blend the mustard, yolk, seasoning and lemon juice, then with the motor running, slowly pour in the oil.

SEAFOOD RICE RING

INGREDIENTS   Serves 4

350 g/12 oz long-grain rice
½ tsp turmeric
5 tbsp sunflower oil
2 tbsp white wine vinegar
1 tsp Dijon mustard
1 tsp caster sugar
1 tbsp mild curry paste
4 shallots, peeled and finely
 chopped
salt and freshly ground black
 pepper

125 g/4 oz peeled prawns,
 thawed if frozen
2 tbsp freshly chopped
 coriander
8 fresh crevettes or large tiger
 prawns, with shells on
4 sprigs of fresh coriander, to
 garnish
lemon wedges, to serve

1 Lightly oil a 1.1 litre/2 pint ring mould, or line the mould with clingfilm. Cook the rice in boiling salted water with the turmeric for 15 minutes, or until tender. Drain thoroughly. Whisk 4 tablespoons of the oil with the vinegar, mustard and sugar to form a dressing and pour over the warm rice. Reserve.

2 Heat the remaining oil in a saucepan, add the curry paste and shallots and cook for 5 minutes, or until the shallots are just softened. Fold into the dressed rice, season to taste with salt and pepper and mix well. Leave to cool completely.

3 Stir in the prawns and the chopped coriander and turn into the prepared ring mould. Press the mixture down firmly with a spoon, then chill in the refrigerator for at least 1 hour.

4 Invert the ring onto a serving plate and fill the centre with the crevettes or tiger prawns. Arrange the cooked mussels around the edge of the ring and garnish with sprigs of fresh coriander. Serve immediately with lemon wedges.

HELPFUL HINT

Make sure that you use ordinary long-grain rice for this seafood ring – easy-cook varieties are pretreated so that the grains remain separate and do not stick together (the opposite of what you require here). A mixture of basmati and wild rice can be used, if preferred.

CHEESY VEGETABLE & PRAWN BAKE

INGREDIENTS   Serves 4

175 g/6 oz long-grain rice
salt and freshly ground black
   pepper
1 garlic clove, peeled and
   crushed
1 large egg, beaten
3 tbsp freshly shredded basil
4 tbsp Parmesan cheese,
   grated
125 g/4 oz baby asparagus
   spears, trimmed

150 g/5 oz baby carrots,
   trimmed
150 g/5 oz fine green beans,
   trimmed
150 g/5 oz cherry tomatoes
175 g/6 oz peeled prawns,
   thawed if frozen
125 g/4 oz mozzarella cheese,
   thinly sliced

1 Preheat the oven to 200°C/
400°F/Gas Mark 6, about 10
minutes before required. Cook the
rice in lightly salted boiling water
for 12–15 minutes, or until
tender, drain. Stir in the garlic,
beaten egg, shredded basil,
2 tablespoons of the Parmesan
cheese and season to taste with
salt and pepper. Press this mixture
into a greased 23 cm/9 inch
square ovenproof dish and reserve.

2 Bring a large saucepan of
water to the boil, then drop
in the asparagus, carrots and
green beans. Return to the boil
and cook for 3–4 minutes. Drain
and leave to cool.

3 Quarter or halve the
cherry tomatoes and mix
them into the cooled vegetables.
Spread the prepared vegetables
over the rice and top with the
prawns. Season to taste with salt
and pepper.

4 Cover the prawns with the
mozzarella and sprinkle over
the remaining Parmesan cheese.
Bake in the preheated oven for
20–25 minutes until piping hot
and golden brown in places.
Serve immediately.

FOOD FACT

Mozzarella is a fresh-tasting
unripened cheese, now
produced throughout Italy.
Traditional mozzarella is
made from buffalo milk, but
cows' milk is commonly used,
or sometimes a mixture of
the two. The cheese becomes
stringy when cooked, so
should be sliced as thinly as
possible here.

FISH CRUMBLE

INGREDIENTS   Serves 6

450 g/1 lb whiting or halibut
fillets
300 ml/½ pint milk
salt and freshly ground black
pepper
1 tbsp sunflower oil
75 g/3 oz butter or margarine
1 medium onion, peeled and
finely chopped
2 leeks, trimmed and sliced
1 medium carrot, peeled and
cut into small dice
2 medium potatoes, peeled
and cut into small pieces

175 g/6 oz plain flour
300 ml/½ pint fish or vegetable
stock
2 tbsp whipping cream
1 tsp freshly chopped dill
runner beans, to serve

FOR THE CRUMBLE TOPPING:
75 g/3 oz butter or margarine
175 g/6 oz plain flour
75 g/3 oz Parmesan cheese,
grated
¾ tsp cayenne pepper

1 Preheat the oven to 200°C/
400°F/Gas Mark 6, 15
minutes before cooking. Oil a
1.4 litre/2½ pint pie dish. Place
the fish in a saucepan with the
milk, salt and pepper. Bring to the
boil, cover and simmer for 8–10
minutes until the fish is cooked.
Remove with a slotted spoon,
reserving the cooking liquid. Flake
the fish into the prepared dish.

2 Heat the oil and 1 tablespoon
of the butter or margarine in
a small frying pan and gently fry
the onion, leeks, carrot and
potatoes for 1–2 minutes. Cover
tightly and cook over a gentle
heat for a further 10 minutes
until softened. Spoon the
vegetables over the fish.

3 Melt the remaining butter or
margarine in a saucepan, add
the flour and cook for 1 minute,
stirring. Whisk in the reserved
cooking liquid and the stock. Cook
until thickened, then stir in the
cream. Remove from the heat and
stir in the dill. Pour over the fish.

4 To make the crumble, rub
the butter or margarine into
the flour until it resembles breadcrumbs, then stir in the cheese and
cayenne pepper. Sprinkle over the
dish, and bake in the preheated
oven for 20 minutes until piping
hot. Serve with runner beans.

TASTY TIP

Vary the taste and texture of
the topping by making it with
wholemeal flour, or by
adding 25 g/1 oz chopped
nuts or jumbo porridge oats.

POTATO BOULANGERE WITH SEA BASS

INGREDIENTS   Serves 2

450 g/1 lb potatoes, peeled
   and thinly sliced
1 large onion, peeled and
   thinly sliced
salt and freshly ground black
   pepper

300 ml/½ pint fish or vegetable
   stock
75 g/3 oz butter or margarine
350 g/12 oz sea bass fillets
sprigs of fresh flat-leaf parsley,
   to garnish

1 Preheat the oven to 200°C/
400°F/Gas Mark 6. Lightly
grease a shallow 1.4 litre/2½ pint
baking dish with oil or butter.
Layer the potato slices and onions
alternately in the prepared dish,
seasoning each layer with salt
and pepper.

2 Pour the stock over the top,
then cut 50 g/2 oz of the
butter or margarine into small
pieces and dot over the top layer.
Bake in the preheated oven for
50–60 minutes. Do not cover the
dish at this stage.

3 Lightly rinse the sea bass
fillets and pat dry on
absorbent kitchen paper. Cook in
a griddle, or heat the remaining
butter or margarine in a frying
pan and shallow fry the fish fillets
for 3–4 minutes per side, flesh
side first. Remove from the pan
with a slotted spatula and drain
on absorbent kitchen paper.

4 Remove the partly cooked
potato and onion mixture

from the oven and place the fish
on the top. Cover with tinfoil
and return to the oven for 10
minutes until heated through.
Garnish with sprigs of parsley
and serve immediately.

FOOD FACT

Sea bass, also known as sea
perch, is a large round fish
which grows up to 1 m/3⅓ ft
long, and may weigh up to 9
kg/20 lb. In appearance, it is
similar to a salmon, but a
much darker grey colour.
Cook it gently and handle it
with care, as the flesh is
soft and delicate.

JAMAICAN JERK PORK WITH RICE & PEAS

INGREDIENTS   Serves 4

175 g/6 oz dried red kidney
  beans, soaked overnight

2 onions, peeled and chopped

2 garlic cloves, peeled and
  crushed

4 tbsp lime juice

2 tbsp each dark molasses,
  soy sauce and chopped fresh
  root ginger

2 jalapeño chillies, deseeded
  and chopped

½ tsp ground cinnamon

¼ tsp each ground allspice,
  ground nutmeg

4 pork loin chops, on the bone

FOR THE RICE:

1 tbsp vegetable oil

1 onion, peeled and finely
  chopped

1 celery stalk, trimmed and
  finely sliced

3 garlic cloves, peeled and
  crushed

2 bay leaves

225 g/8 oz long-grain white
  rice

475 ml/18 fl oz chicken or ham
  stock

sprigs of fresh flat-leaf parsley,
  to garnish

1 To make the jerk pork marinade, purée the onions, garlic, lime juice, molasses, soy sauce, ginger, chillies, cinnamon, allspice and nutmeg together in a food processor until smooth. Put the pork chops into a plastic or non-reactive dish and pour over the marinade, turning the chops to coat. Marinate in the refrigerator for at least 1 hour or overnight.

2 Drain the beans and place in a large saucepan with about 2 litres/3½ pints cold water. Bring to the boil and boil rapidly for 10 minutes. Reduce the heat, cover and simmer gently, for 1 hour until tender, adding more water, if necessary. When cooked, drain well and mash roughly.

3 Heat the oil for the rice in a saucepan with a tight-fitting lid and add the onion, celery and garlic. Cook gently for 5 minutes until softened. Add the bay leaves, rice and stock and stir. Bring to the boil, cover and cook very gently for 10 minutes. Add the beans and stir well again. Cook for a further 5 minutes, then remove from the heat.

4 Heat a griddle pan until almost smoking. Remove the pork chops from the marinade, scraping off any surplus and add to the hot pan. Cook for 5–8 minutes on each side, or until cooked. Garnish with the parsley and serve immediately with the rice.

PORK LOIN STUFFED WITH ORANGE & HAZELNUT RICE

INGREDIENTS

Serves 4

15 g/½ oz butter
1 shallot, peeled and finely
    chopped
50 g/2 oz long-grain brown
    rice
175 ml/6 fl oz vegetable stock
½ orange
25 g/1 oz ready-to-eat dried
    prunes, stoned and chopped
25 g/1 oz hazelnuts, roasted
    and roughly chopped

1 small egg, beaten
1 tbsp freshly chopped parsley
salt and freshly ground pepper
450 g/1 lb boneless pork
    tenderloin or fillet, trimmed

FOR THE RICE:
steamed courgettes
carrots

1 Preheat the oven to 190°C/ 375°F/Gas Mark 5, 10 minutes before required. Heat the butter in a small saucepan, add the shallot and cook gently for 2–3 minutes until softened. Add the rice and stir well for 1 minute. Add the stock, stir well and bring to the boil. Cover tightly and simmer gently for 30 minutes until the rice is tender and all the liquid is absorbed. Leave to cool.

2 Grate the orange rind and reserve. Remove the white pith and chop the orange flesh finely. Mix together the orange rind and flesh, prunes, hazelnuts, cooled rice, egg and parsley. Season to taste with salt and pepper.

3 Cut the fillet in half, then using a sharp knife, split the pork fillet lengthways almost in two, forming a pocket, leaving

it just attached. Open out the pork and put between 2 pieces of clingfilm. Flatten using a meat mallet until about half its original thickness. Spoon the filling into the pocket and close the fillet over. Tie along the length with kitchen string at regular intervals.

4 Put the pork fillet in a small roasting tray and cook in the top of the preheated oven for 25–30 minutes, or until the meat is just tender. Remove from the oven and allow to rest for 5 minutes. Slice into rounds and serve with steamed courgettes and carrots.

TASTY TIP

For an alternative stuffing try adding pine nuts and thyme.

PORK GOULASH & RICE

INGREDIENTS   Serves 4

700 g/1½ lb boneless pork rib
  chops
1 tbsp olive oil
2 onions, peeled and roughly
  chopped
1 red pepper, deseeded and
  sliced thinly
1 garlic clove, peeled and
  crushed
1 tbsp plain flour

1 rounded tbsp paprika
400 g can chopped tomatoes
salt and freshly ground black
  pepper
250 g/9 oz long-grain white rice
450 ml/¾ pint chicken stock
sprigs of fresh flat-leaf parsley,
  to garnish
150 ml/¼ pint soured cream, to
  serve

1 Preheat the oven to 140°C/
275°F/Gas Mark 1. Cut the
pork into large cubes, about
4 cm/1½ inches square. Heat the
oil in a large flameproof casserole
and brown the pork in batches
over a high heat, transferring the
cubes to a plate as they brown.

2 Over a medium heat, add the
onions and pepper and cook
for about 5 minutes, stirring
regularly, until they begin to
brown. Add the garlic and return
the meat to the casserole along
with any juices on the plate.
Sprinkle in the flour and paprika
and stir well to soak up the oil
and juices.

3 Add the tomatoes and season
to taste with salt and pepper.
Bring slowly to the boil, cover
with a tight-fitting lid and cook in
the preheated oven for 1½ hours.

4 Meanwhile, rinse the rice in
several changes of water until
the water remains relatively clear.
Drain well and put into a
saucepan with the chicken stock
or water and a little salt. Cover
tightly and bring to the boil.
Turn the heat down as low as
possible and cook for 10 minutes
without removing the lid. After
10 minutes, remove from the
heat and leave for a further 10
minutes, without removing the
lid. Fluff with a fork.

5 When the meat is tender, stir
in the soured cream lightly to
create a marbled effect, or serve
separately. Garnish with parsley and
serve immediately with the rice.

FOOD FACT

Paprika is the ground red
powder from the dried
pepper *Capsicum annum*
and is a vital ingredient of
goulash, giving it a distinctive
colour and taste.

LAMB PILAF

INGREDIENTS

Serves 4

2 tbsp vegetable oil

25 g/1 oz flaked or slivered almonds

1 medium onion, peeled and finely chopped

1 medium carrot, peeled and finely chopped

1 celery stalk, trimmed and finely chopped

350 g/12 oz lean lamb, cut into chunks

¼ tsp ground cinnamon

¼ tsp chilli flakes

2 large tomatoes, skinned, deseeded and chopped

grated rind of 1 orange

350 g/12 oz easy-cook brown basmati rice

600 ml/1 pint vegetable or lamb stock

2 tbsp freshly snipped chives

3 tbsp freshly chopped coriander

salt and freshly ground black pepper

TO GARNISH:

lemon slices

sprigs of fresh coriander

1 Preheat the oven to 140°C/ 275°F/Gas Mark 1. Heat the oil in a flameproof casserole with a tight-fitting lid and add the almonds. Cook for about 1 minute until just starting to brown, stirring often. Add the onion, carrot and celery and cook gently for a further 8–10 minutes until soft and lightly browned.

2 Increase the heat and add the lamb. Cook for a further 5 minutes until the lamb has changed colour. Add the ground cinnamon and chilli flakes and stir briefly before adding the tomatoes and orange rind.

3 Stir and add the rice, then the stock. Bring slowly to the boil and cover tightly. Transfer to the preheated oven and cook for 30–35 minutes until the rice is tender and the stock is absorbed.

4 Remove from the oven and leave to stand for 5 minutes before stirring in the chives and coriander. Season to taste with salt and pepper. Garnish with the lemon slices and sprigs of fresh coriander and serve immediately.

TASTY TIP

The lamb in this aromatic pilaf is cooked for a relatively short time, so choose a tender cut such as leg, shoulder or fillet. If you buy the meat on the bone, use the bones to make a stock – it will make all the difference to the final flavour of the dish.

NASI GORENG

INGREDIENTS   Serves 4

7 large shallots, peeled

1 red chilli, deseeded and roughly chopped

2 garlic cloves, peeled and roughly chopped

4 tbsp sunflower oil

2 tsp each tomato purée and Indonesian sweet soy sauce (katjap manis)

225 g/8 oz long-grain white rice

125 g/4 oz French beans, trimmed

3 medium eggs, beaten

pinch of sugar

salt and freshly ground black pepper

225 g/8 oz cooked ham, shredded

225 g/8 oz cooked peeled prawns, thawed if frozen

6 spring onions, trimmed and thinly sliced

1 tbsp light soy sauce

3 tbsp freshly chopped coriander

1 Roughly chop 1 of the shallots and place with the red chilli, garlic, 1 tablespoon of the oil, tomato purée and sweet soy sauce in a food processor and blend until smooth, then reserve. Boil the rice in plenty of salted water for 6–7 minutes until tender, adding the French beans after 4 minutes. Drain well and leave to cool.

2 Beat the eggs with the sugar and a little salt and pepper. Heat a little of the oil in a small non-stick frying pan and add about one-third of the egg mixture. Swirl to coat the base of the pan thinly and cook for about 1 minute until golden. Flip and cook the other side briefly before removing from the pan. Roll the omelette and slice thinly into strips. Repeat with the remaining egg to make 3 omelettes.

3 Thinly slice the remaining shallots then heat a further 2 tablespoons of the oil in a clean frying pan. Add the shallots to the pan and cook for 8–10 minutes over a medium heat until golden and crisp. Drain on absorbent kitchen paper and reserve.

4 Add the remaining 1 tablespoon of oil to a large wok or frying pan and fry the chilli paste over a medium heat for 1 minute. Add the cooked rice and beans and stir-fry for 2 minutes. Add the ham and prawns and continue stir-frying for a further 1–2 minutes. Add the omelette slices, half the fried shallots, the spring onions, soy sauce and chopped coriander. Stir-fry for a further minute until heated through. Spoon onto serving plates and garnish with the remaining crispy shallots. Serve immediately.

LEEK & HAM RISOTTO

INGREDIENTS
Serves 4

1 tbsp olive oil
25 g/1 oz butter
1 medium onion, peeled and
   finely chopped
4 leeks, trimmed and thinly
   sliced
1½ tbsp freshly chopped
   thyme
350 g/12 oz Arborio rice

1.4 litres/2¼ pints vegetable or
   chicken stock, heated
225 g/8 oz cooked ham
175 g/6 oz peas, thawed if
   frozen
50 g/2 oz Parmesan cheese,
   grated
salt and freshly ground black
   pepper

1 Heat the oil and half the butter together in a large saucepan. Add the onion and leeks and cook over a medium heat for 6–8 minutes, stirring occasionally, until soft and beginning to colour. Stir in the thyme and cook briefly.

2 Add the rice and stir well. Continue stirring over a medium heat for about 1 minute until the rice is glossy. Add a ladleful or two of the stock and stir well until the stock is absorbed. Continue adding stock, a ladleful at a time, and stirring well between additions, until about two-thirds of the stock has been added.

3 Meanwhile, either chop or finely shred the ham, then add to the saucepan of rice together with the peas. Continue adding ladlefuls of stock, as described in step 2, until the rice is tender and the ham is heated through thoroughly.

4 Add the remaining butter, sprinkle over the Parmesan cheese and season to taste with salt and pepper. When the butter has melted and the cheese has softened, stir well to incorporate. Taste and adjust the seasoning, then serve immediately.

HELPFUL HINT

Risotto should take about 15 minutes to cook, so taste it after this time – the rice should be creamy with just a slight bite to it. If it is not quite ready, continue adding the stock, a little at a time, and cook for a few more minutes. Stop as soon as it tastes ready as you do not have to add all of the liquid.

ROAST LEG OF LAMB & BOULANGERE POTATOES

INGREDIENTS   Serves 6

1.1 kg/2½ lb potatoes, peeled
1 large onion, peeled and
   finely sliced
salt and freshly ground black
   pepper
2 tbsp olive oil
50 g/2 oz butter
200 ml/7 fl oz lamb stock

100 ml/3½ fl oz milk
2 kg/4½ lb leg of lamb
2–3 sprigs of fresh rosemary
6 large garlic cloves, peeled
   and finely sliced
6 anchovy fillets, drained
extra sprigs of fresh rosemary,
   to garnish

1 Preheat the oven to 230°C/ 450°F/Gas Mark 8. Finely slice the potatoes – a mandolin is the best tool for this. Layer the potatoes with the onion in a large roasting tin, seasoning each layer with salt and pepper. Drizzle about 1 tablespoon of the olive oil over the potatoes and add the butter in small pieces. Pour in the lamb stock and milk. Set aside.

2 Make small incisions all over the lamb with the point of a small, sharp knife. Into each incision insert a small piece of rosemary, a sliver of garlic and a piece of anchovy fillet.

3 Drizzle the leg of lamb and its flavourings with the rest of the olive oil and season well. Place the meat directly onto a shelf in the preheated oven. Position the roasting tin of potatoes directly underneath to catch the juices during cooking. Roast for 15 minutes per 500 g/ 1 lb 2 oz (about 1 hour for a joint this

size), reducing the oven temperature after 20 minutes to 200°C/ 400°F/Gas Mark 6.

4 When the lamb is cooked, remove from the oven and allow to rest for 10 minutes before carving. Meanwhile, increase the oven heat and cook the potatoes for a further 10–15 minutes to crisp up. Garnish with fresh rosemary sprigs and serve immediately with the lamb.

FOOD FACT

Leg of lamb is one of the prime roasting joints and is known by its French name *gigot* in Scotland. It may weigh between 1.8–2.7 kg/ 4–6 lb, so ask for a small joint for this dish. Although home-produced lamb is at its best in the spring, there is a good supply all year round of imported New Zealand lamb.

LANCASHIRE HOTPOT

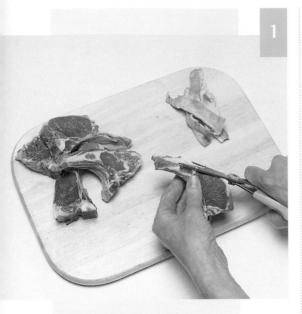

INGREDIENTS   Serves 4

1 kg/2¼ lb middle end neck of
  lamb, divided into cutlets
2 tbsp vegetable oil
2 large onions, peeled and
  sliced
2 tsp plain flour
150 ml/¼ pint vegetable or
  lamb stock
700 g/1½ lb waxy potatoes,
  peeled and thickly sliced

salt and freshly ground black
  pepper
1 bay leaf
2 sprigs of fresh thyme
1 tbsp melted butter
2 tbsp freshly chopped herbs,
  to garnish
freshly cooked green beans,
  to serve

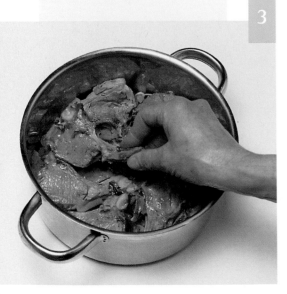

1 Preheat the oven to 170°C/ 325°F/Gas Mark 3. Trim any excess fat from the lamb cutlets. Heat the oil in a frying pan and brown the cutlets in batches for 3–4 minutes. Remove with a slotted spoon and reserve. Add the onions to the frying pan and cook for 6–8 minutes until softened and just beginning to colour, then remove and reserve.

2 Stir in the flour and cook for a few seconds, then gradually pour in the stock, stirring well, and bring to the boil. Remove from the heat.

3 Spread the base of a large casserole with half the potato slices. Top with half the onions and season well with salt and pepper. Arrange the browned meat in a layer. Season again and add the remaining onions, bay leaf and thyme. Pour in the remaining liquid from the onions and top with remaining potatoes

so that they overlap in a single layer. Brush the potatoes with the melted butter and season again.

4 Cover the saucepan and cook in the preheated oven for 2 hours, uncovering for the last 30 minutes to allow the potatoes to brown. Garnish with chopped herbs and serve immediately with green beans.

FOOD FACT

The name of this classic dish derives from the past tradition of wrapping it in blankets after cooking to keep it warm until lunchtime. There are dozens of versions all claiming to be authentic. Some include lambs kidneys to enrich the gravy, but whatever the ingredients, it is important to season well and to cook it slowly, so that the lamb is meltingly tender.

SHEPHERD'S PIE

INGREDIENTS   Serves 4

2 tbsp vegetable or olive oil

1 onion, peeled and finely chopped

1 carrot, peeled and finely chopped

1 celery stalk, trimmed and finely chopped

1 tbsp sprigs of fresh thyme

450 g/1 lb leftover roast lamb, finely chopped

150 ml/¼ pint red wine

150 ml/¼ pint lamb or

vegetable stock or leftover gravy

2 tbsp tomato purée

salt and freshly ground black pepper

700 g/1½ lb potatoes, peeled and cut into chunks

25 g/1 oz butter

6 tbsp milk

1 tbsp freshly chopped parsley

fresh herbs, to garnish

1 Preheat the oven to 200°C/ 400°F/Gas Mark 6, about 15 minutes before cooking. Heat the oil in a large saucepan and add the onion, carrot and celery. Cook over a medium heat for 8–10 minutes until softened and starting to brown.

2 Add the thyme and cook briefly, then add the cooked lamb, wine, stock and tomato purée. Season to taste with salt and pepper and simmer gently for 25–30 minutes until reduced and thickened. Remove from the heat to cool slightly and season again.

3 Meanwhile, boil the potatoes in plenty of salted water for 12–15 minutes until tender. Drain and return to the saucepan over a low heat to dry out. Remove from the heat and add the butter, milk and parsley. Mash until creamy, adding a little

more milk, if necessary. Adjust the seasoning.

4 Transfer the lamb mixture to a shallow ovenproof dish. Spoon the mash over the filling and spread evenly to cover completely. Fork the surface, place on a baking sheet, then cook in the preheated oven for 25–30 minutes until the potato topping is browned and the filling is piping hot. Garnish and serve.

TASTY TIP

A traditional Shepherds pie is always made from cold roast lamb, but you can make it with fresh minced lamb if preferred. Simply dry-fry 450 g/ 1 lb lean mince in a non-stick frying pan over a high heat until well-browned, then follow the recipe as before.

CORNISH PASTIES

INGREDIENTS   Makes 8

FOR THE PASTRY:
350 g/12 oz self-raising flour
75 g/3 oz butter or margarine
75 g/3 oz lard or white
  vegetable fat
salt and freshly ground black
  pepper

1 large onion, peeled and
  finely chopped
1 large potato, peeled and diced
200 g/7 oz swede, peeled and
  diced
3 tbsp Worcestershire sauce
1 small egg, beaten, to glaze

FOR THE FILLING:
550 g/1¼ lb braising steak,
  chopped very finely

TO GARNISH:
tomato slices or wedges
sprigs of fresh parsley

1 Preheat the oven to 180°C/
350°F/Gas Mark 4, about 15
minutes before required. To make
the pastry, sift the flour into a
large bowl and add the fats,
chopped into little pieces. Rub
the fats and flour together until
the mixture resembles coarse
breadcrumbs. Season to taste with
salt and pepper and mix again.

2 Add about 2 tablespoons of
cold water, a little at a time,
and mix until the mixture comes
together to form a firm but
pliable dough. Turn onto a lightly
floured surface, knead until
smooth, then wrap and chill in
the refrigerator.

3 To make the filling, put
the braising steak in a large
bowl with the onion. Add the
potatoes and swede to the bowl
together with the Worcestershire
sauce and salt and pepper.
Mix well.

4 Divide the dough into 8 balls
and roll each ball into a circle
about 25.5 cm/10 inches across.
Divide the filling between the
circles of pastry. Wet the edge of
the pastry, then fold over the
filling. Pinch the edges to seal.

5 Transfer the pasties to a lightly
oiled baking sheet. Make a
couple of small holes in each pasty
and brush with beaten egg. Cook
in the preheated oven for 15
minutes, remove and brush again
with the egg. Return to the oven
for a further 15–20 minutes until
golden. Cool slightly, garnish with
tomato and parsley and serve.

TASTY TIP

The shortcrust pastry for
these pasties is made with
self-raising flour, which gives
it a softer, lighter texture.

SEARED CALVES' LIVER WITH ONIONS & MUSTARD MASH

INGREDIENTS   Serves 2

2 tbsp olive oil
100 g/3½ oz butter
3 large onions, peeled and
 finely sliced
pinch of sugar
salt and freshly ground black
 pepper
1 tbsp sprigs of fresh thyme
1 tbsp balsamic vinegar

700 g/1½ lb potatoes, peeled
 and cut into chunks
6–8 tbsp milk
1 tbsp wholegrain mustard
3–4 fresh sage leaves
550 g/1¼ lb thinly sliced
 calves' liver
1 tsp lemon juice

1 Preheat the oven to 150°C/ 300°F/Gas Mark 2. Heat half the oil and 25 g/1 oz of the butter in a flameproof casserole. When foaming, add the onions. Cover and cook over a low heat for 20 minutes until softened and beginning to collapse. Add the sugar and season with salt and pepper. Stir in the thyme. Cover the casserole and transfer to the preheated oven. Cook for a further 30–45 minutes until softened completely, but not browned. Remove from the oven and stir in the balsamic vinegar.

2 Meanwhile, boil the potatoes in boiling salted water for 15–18 minutes until tender. Drain well, then return to the pan. Place over a low heat to dry completely, remove from the heat and stir in 50 g/2 oz of the butter, the milk, mustard and salt and pepper to taste. Mash thoroughly until creamy and keep warm.

3 Heat a large frying pan and add the remaining butter and oil. When it is foaming, add the mustard and sage leaves and stir for a few seconds, then add the liver. Cook over a high heat for 1–2 minutes on each side. It should remain slightly pink: do not overcook. Remove the liver from the pan. Add the lemon juice to the pan and swirl around to deglaze.

4 To serve, place a large spoonful of the mashed potato on each plate. Top with some of the melting onions, the liver and finally the pan juices.

HELPFUL HINT

Calves' liver is mild and tender and needs only brief cooking over a high heat to sear the outside, but keep it moist and juicy within.

RED WINE RISOTTO WITH LAMBS' KIDNEYS & CARAMELISED SHALLOTS

INGREDIENTS   Serves 4

8 lambs' kidneys, halved and
  cores removed
150 ml/¼ pint milk
2 tbsp olive oil
50 g/2 oz butter
275 g/10 oz shallots, peeled
  and halved if large
1 onion, peeled and finely
  chopped
2 garlic cloves, peeled and
  finely chopped

350 g/12 oz Arborio rice
225 ml/8 fl oz red wine
1 litre/1¾ pints chicken or
  vegetable stock, heated
1 tbsp sprigs of fresh thyme
50 g/2 oz Parmesan cheese,
  grated
salt and freshly ground black
  pepper
fresh herbs, to garnish

1 Place the lambs' kidneys in a bowl and pour the milk over. Leave to soak for 15–20 minutes, then drain and pat dry on absorbent kitchen paper. Discard the milk.

2 Heat 1 tablespoon of the oil with 25 g/1 oz of the butter in a medium saucepan. Add the shallots, cover and cook for 10 minutes over a gentle heat. Remove the lid and cook for a further 10 minutes, or until tender and golden.

3 Meanwhile, heat the remaining oil with the remaining butter in a deep-sided frying pan. Add the onion and cook over a medium heat for 5–7 minutes until starting to brown. Add the garlic and cook briefly.

4 Stir in the rice and cook for a further minute until glossy and well coated in oil and butter. Add half the red wine and stir until absorbed. Add a ladleful or two of the stock and stir well until the stock is absorbed. Continue adding the stock, a ladleful at a time, and stirring well between additions, until all of the stock is added and the rice is just tender, but still firm. Remove from the heat.

5 Meanwhile, when the rice is nearly cooked, increase the heat under the shallots, add the thyme and kidneys. Cook for 3–4 minutes, then add the wine.

6 Bring to the boil, then simmer rapidly until the red wine is reduced and syrupy. Stir the cheese into the rice with the caramelised shallots and kidneys. Season to taste, garnish and serve.

MARINATED LAMB CHOPS WITH GARLIC FRIED POTATOES

INGREDIENTS

Serves 4

4 thick lamb chump chops
3 tbsp olive oil
550 g/1¼ lb potatoes, peeled
   and cut into 1 cm/½ inch dice
6 unpeeled garlic cloves
mixed salad or freshly cooked
   vegetables, to serve

FOR THE MARINADE:
1 small bunch of fresh thyme,
   leaves removed
1 tbsp freshly chopped
   rosemary
1 tsp salt
2 garlic cloves, peeled and
   crushed
rind and juice of 1 lemon
2 tbsp olive oil

1 Trim the chops of any excess fat, wipe with a clean damp cloth and reserve. To make the marinade, using a pestle and mortar, pound the thyme leaves and rosemary with the salt until pulpy. Add the garlic and continue pounding until crushed. Stir in the lemon rind and juice and the olive oil.

2 Pour the marinade over the lamb chops, turning them until they are well coated. Cover lightly and leave to marinate in the refrigerator for about 1 hour.

3 Meanwhile, heat the oil in a large non-stick frying pan. Add the potatoes and garlic and cook over a low heat for about 20 minutes, stirring occasionally. Increase the heat and cook for a further 10–15 minutes until golden. Drain on absorbent

kitchen paper and add salt to taste. Keep warm.

4 Heat a griddle pan until almost smoking. Add the lamb chops and cook for 3–4 minutes on each side until golden, but still pink in the middle. Serve with the potatoes, and either a mixed salad or freshly cooked vegetables.

TASTY TIP

Marinating the chops not only adds flavour, but tenderises as well, due to the acids in the lemon juice. If time allows, marinate the chops for slightly longer. Try other citrus juices in this recipe for a change. Both orange and lime juice would be delicious.

PORK SAUSAGES WITH ONION GRAVY & BEST-EVER MASH

INGREDIENTS   Serves 4

50 g/2 oz butter
1 tbsp olive oil
2 large onions, peeled and
   thinly sliced
pinch of sugar
1 tbsp freshly chopped thyme
1 tbsp plain flour
100 ml/3½ fl oz Madeira
200 ml/7 fl oz vegetable stock
8–12 good-quality butchers
   pork sausages, depending
   on size

FOR THE MASH:
900 g/2 lb floury potatoes,
   peeled
75 g/3 oz butter
4 tbsp crème fraîche or soured
   cream
salt and freshly ground black
   pepper

1 Melt the butter with the oil and add the onions. Cover and cook gently for about 20 minutes until the onions have collapsed. Add the sugar and stir well. Uncover and continue to cook, stirring often, until the onions are very soft and golden. Add the thyme, stir well, then add the flour, stirring. Gradually add the Madeira and the stock. Bring to the boil and simmer gently for 10 minutes.

2 Meanwhile, put the sausages in a large frying pan and cook over a medium heat for about 15–20 minutes, turning often, until golden brown and slightly sticky all over.

3 For the mash, boil the potatoes in plenty of lightly salted water for 15–18 minutes until tender. Drain well and return to the saucepan. Put the saucepan over a low heat to allow the potatoes to dry thoroughly. Remove from the heat and add the butter, crème fraîche and salt and pepper. Mash thoroughly. Serve the potato mash topped with the sausages and onion gravy.

HELPFUL HINT

Sausages should always be cooked slowly over a gentle heat to ensure that they are cooked through. There is a huge range of regional pork sausages to choose from. Try meaty Cambridge sausages packed with herbs and spices, or Cumberland sausages made form coarsely chopped pork and black pepper.

CHILLI CON CARNE WITH CRISPY-SKINNED POTATOES

INGREDIENTS   Serves 4

2 tbsp vegetable oil, plus extra
  for brushing
1 large onion, peeled and
  finely chopped
1 garlic clove, peeled and
  finely chopped
1 red chilli, deseeded and
  finely chopped
450 g/1 lb chuck steak, finely
  chopped, or lean beef mince
1 tbsp chilli powder

400 g can chopped tomatoes
2 tbsp tomato purée
400 g can red kidney beans,
  drained and rinsed
4 large baking potatoes
coarse salt and freshly ground
  black pepper

TO SERVE:
ready-made guacamole
soured cream

1 Preheat the oven to 150°C/
300°F/Gas Mark 2. Heat the
oil in a large flameproof casserole
and add the onion. Cook gently
for 10 minutes until soft and
lightly browned. Add the garlic
and chilli and cook briefly.
Increase the heat. Add the chuck
steak or lean mince and cook for
a further 10 minutes, stirring
occasionally, until browned.

2 Add the chilli powder and
stir well. Cook for about 2
minutes, then add the chopped
tomatoes and tomato purée.
Bring slowly to the boil. Cover
and cook in the preheated oven
for 1½ hours. Remove from the
oven and stir in the kidney beans.
Return to the oven for a further
15 minutes.

3 Meanwhile, brush a little
vegetable oil all over the

potatoes and rub on some coarse
salt. Put the potatoes in the oven
alongside the chilli.

4 Remove the chilli and
potatoes from the oven.
Cut a cross in each potato, then
squeeze to open slightly and
season to taste with salt and
pepper. Serve with the chilli,
guacamole and soured cream.

TASTY TIP

Make your own guacamole
by peeling, stoning and
mashing 1 large avocado in a
bowl with 2 tablespoons each
of lemon juice and crème
fraîche, ¼ teaspoon Tabasco
sauce, 1 crushed garlic clove
and salt and pepper. Push the
avocado stone into the dip to
stop it from discolouring.

ROAST CURED PORK LOIN WITH BAKED SLICED POTATOES

INGREDIENTS   Serves 4

2 tbsp wholegrain mustard
2 tbsp clear honey
1 tsp coarsely crushed black
  pepper
900 g/2 lb piece smoked cured
  pork loin
900 g/2 lb potatoes, peeled
  and thinly sliced

75 g/3 oz butter, diced
1 large onion, peeled and
  finely chopped
25 g/1 oz plain flour
salt and freshly ground black
  pepper
600 ml/1 pint milk
fresh green salad, to serve

1 Preheat the oven to 190°C/
375°F/Gas Mark 5. Mix
together the mustard, honey
and black pepper. Spread evenly
over the pork loin. Place in the
centre of a large square of tinfoil
and wrap loosely. Cook in the
preheated oven for 15 minutes
per 450 g/1 lb, plus an extra
15 minutes (45 minutes),
unwrapping the joint for the
last 30 minutes cooking time.

2 Meanwhile, layer one-third
of the potatoes, one-third of
the butter, half the onions and
half the flour in a large gratin
dish. Add half the remaining
potatoes and butter and the
remaining onions and flour.
Finally, cover with the remaining
potatoes. Season well with salt
and pepper between layers. Pour
in the milk and dot with the
remaining butter. Cover the dish
loosely with tinfoil and put in the
oven below the pork. Cook for
1½ hours.

3 Remove the tinfoil from the
potatoes and cook for a
further 20 minutes until tender
and golden. Remove the pork
loin from the oven and leave to
rest for 10 minutes before carving
thinly. Serve with the potatoes
and a fresh green salad.

HELPFUL HINT

Smoked cured pork loin can
be found in specialist
butchers and is delicately
flavoured. If you are unable to
find it, an ordinary piece of
pork loin can be used here. It
usually has a good layer of
crackling, so remove it for
this recipe, sprinkle with a
little salt and cook separately
under the grill.

GRILLED STEAKS WITH SAFFRON POTATOES & ROAST TOMATOES

INGREDIENTS

Serves 4

700 g/1½ lb new potatoes, halved

few strands of saffron

300 ml/½ pint vegetable or beef stock

1 small onion, peeled and finely chopped

75 g/3 oz butter

salt and freshly ground black pepper

2 tsp balsamic vinegar

2 tbsp olive oil

1 tsp caster sugar

8 plum tomatoes, halved

4 boneless sirloin steaks, each weighing 225 g/8 oz

2 tbsp freshly chopped parsley

1 Cook the potatoes in boiling salted water for 8 minutes and drain well. Return the potatoes to the saucepan along with the saffron, stock, onion and 25 g/1 oz of the butter. Season to taste with salt and pepper and simmer, uncovered for 10 minutes until the potatoes are tender.

2 Meanwhile, preheat the grill to medium. Mix together the vinegar, olive oil, sugar and seasoning. Arrange the tomatoes cut-side up in a foil-lined grill pan and drizzle over the dressing. Grill for 12–15 minutes, basting occasionally, until tender.

3 Melt the remaining butter in a frying pan. Add the steaks and cook for 4–8 minutes to taste and depending on thickness.

4 Arrange the potatoes and tomatoes in the centre of

4 serving plates. Top with the steaks along with any pan juices. Sprinkle over the parsley and serve immediately.

HELPFUL HINT

You can tell how well a steak is cooked by lightly pressing with your fingertips – the less the resistance the rarer the meat. Timing depends on the thickness rather than the weight of the steak. As a rough guide a 2 cm/¾ inch thick steak will take about 2 minutes on each side for rare, 3–4 minutes on each side for medium and 6–7 minutes on each side for well-done.

OSSOBUCO WITH SAFFRON RISOTTO

INGREDIENTS   Serves 4

125 g/4 oz butter
2 tbsp olive oil
4 large pieces of shin of veal
(often sold as ossobuco)
2 onions, peeled and roughly
chopped
2 garlic cloves, peeled and
finely chopped
300 ml/½ pint white wine
5 plum tomatoes, peeled and
chopped

1 tbsp tomato purée
salt and freshly ground black
pepper
2 tbsp freshly chopped parsley
grated rind of 1 small lemon
few strands of saffron, crushed
350 g/12 oz Arborio rice
1.3 litres/2¼ pints chicken
stock, heated
50 g/2 oz Parmesan cheese,
grated

1 Heat 50 g/2 oz butter with half the oil in a large saucepan and add the pieces of veal. Brown lightly on both sides, then transfer to a plate. Add half the onion and garlic and cook gently for about 10 minutes until the onion is just golden.

2 Return the veal to the saucepan along with the white wine, tomatoes and tomato purée. Season lightly with salt and pepper, cover and bring to a gentle simmer. Cook very gently for 1 hour. Uncover and cook for a further 30 minutes until the meat is cooked and the sauce is reduced and thickened. Season to taste. Mix together the remaining garlic, parsley and lemon rind and reserve.

3 Meanwhile, slowly melt the remaining butter and oil in a large deep-sided frying pan. Add the remaining onion and cook gently for 5–7 minutes until just brown. Add the saffron and stir for a few seconds, then add the rice. Cook for a further minute until the rice is well coated in oil and butter.

5 Begin adding the stock a ladleful at a time, stirring well after each addition of stock and waiting until it is absorbed before adding the next. Continue in this way until all the stock is used. Remove from the heat and stir in the grated Parmesan cheese and seasoning.

6 Spoon a little of the saffron risotto onto each of 4 serving plates. Top with the ossobuco and sauce and sprinkle over the reserved garlic and parsley mixture. Serve immediately.

SPANISH-STYLE PORK STEW WITH SAFFRON RICE

INGREDIENTS   Serves 4

2 tbsp olive oil
900 g/2 lb boneless pork
  shoulder, diced
1 large onion, peeled and
  sliced
2 garlic cloves, peeled and
  finely chopped
1 tbsp plain flour
450 g/1 lb plum tomatoes,
  peeled and chopped
175 ml/6 fl oz red wine
1 tbsp freshly chopped basil
1 green pepper, deseeded and
  sliced
50 g/2 oz pimiento-stuffed
  olives, cut in half crossways

salt and freshly ground black
  pepper
fresh basil leaves, to garnish

FOR THE SAFFRON RICE:

1 tbsp olive oil
25 g/1 oz butter
1 small onion, peeled and
  finely chopped
few strands of saffron, crushed
250 g/9 oz long-grain white
  rice
600 ml/1 pint chicken stock

1 Preheat the oven to 150°C/
300°F/Gas Mark 2. Heat the
oil in a large flameproof casserole
and add the pork in batches. Fry
over a high heat until browned.
Transfer to a plate until all the
pork is browned.

2 Lower the heat and add
the onion to the casserole.
Cook for a further 5 minutes
until soft and starting to brown.
Add the garlic and stir briefly
before returning the pork to the
casserole. Add the flour and stir.

3 Add the tomatoes. Gradually
stir in the red wine and add
the basil. Bring to simmering point
and cover. Transfer the casserole

to the lower part of the preheated
oven and cook for 1½ hours. Stir
in the green pepper and olives
and cook for 30 minutes. Season
to taste with salt and pepper.

4 Meanwhile, to make the
saffron rice, heat the oil with
the butter in a saucepan. Add the
onion and cook for 5 minutes
over a medium heat until
softened. Add the saffron and
rice and stir well. Add the stock,
bring to the boil, cover and
reduce the heat as low as possible.
Cook for 15 minutes, covered,
until the rice is tender and the
stock is absorbed. Adjust the
seasoning and serve with the
stew, garnished with fresh basil.

BEEF TERIYAKI WITH GREEN & BLACK RICE

INGREDIENTS   Serves 4

3 tbsp sake (Japanese rice wine)

3 tbsp dry sherry

3 tbsp dark soy sauce

1½ tbsp soft brown sugar

4 sirloin steaks, each weighing 175 g /6 oz, trimmed

350 g/12 oz long-grain and wild rice

2.5 cm/1 inch piece fresh root ginger

225 g/8 oz mangetout

salt

6 spring onions, trimmed and cut into fine strips

1 In a small saucepan, gently heat the sake, dry sherry, dark soy sauce and sugar until the sugar has dissolved. Increase the heat and bring to the boil. Remove from the heat and leave until cold. Lightly wipe the steaks, place in a shallow dish and pour the sake mixture over. Cover loosely and leave to marinate in the refrigerator for at least 1 hour, spooning the marinade over the steaks occasionally.

2 Cook the rice with the piece of root ginger, according to the packet instructions. Drain well, then remove and discard the piece of ginger.

3 Slice the mangetout thinly lengthways into fine shreds. Plunge into a saucepan of boiling salted water, return the water to the boil and drain immediately. Stir the drained mangetout and spring onions into the hot rice.

4 Meanwhile, heat a griddle pan until almost smoking. Remove the steaks from the marinade and cook on the hot grill pan for 3–4 minutes each side, depending on the thickness.

5 Place the remaining marinade in a saucepan and bring to the boil. Simmer rapidly for 2 minutes and remove from the heat. When the steaks are cooked to personal preference, leave to rest for 2–3 minutes, then slice thinly and serve with the rice and the hot marinade.

FOOD FACT

Before 1867, meat was prohibited in Japan in the belief that it would prevent aggression. The Japanese still eat a relatively small amount of meat and tend to use quick-cook tender cuts in dishes.

CHICKEN BASQUAISE

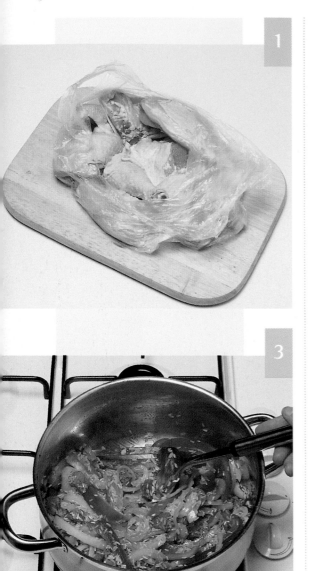

INGREDIENTS   Serves 4–6

1.4 kg/3 lb chicken, cut into 8
   pieces
2 tbsp plain flour
salt and freshly ground black
   pepper
3 tbsp olive oil
1 large onion, peeled and
   sliced
2 red peppers, deseeded and
   cut into thick strips
2 garlic cloves, peeled and
   crushed

150 g/5 oz spicy chorizo
   sausage cut into 1 cm/½ inch
   pieces
200 g/7 oz long-grain white
   rice
450 ml/¾ pint chicken stock
1 tsp crushed dried chillies
½ tsp dried thyme
1 tbsp tomato purée
125 g/4 oz Spanish air-dried
   ham, diced
12 black olives
2 tbsp freshly chopped parsley

1 Dry the chicken pieces well with absorbent kitchen paper. Put the flour in a polythene bag, season with salt and pepper and add the chicken pieces. Twist the bag to seal, then shake to coat the chicken pieces thoroughly.

2 Heat 2 tablespoons of the oil in a large heavy-based saucepan over a medium-high heat. Add the chicken pieces and cook for about 15 minutes, turning on all sides, until well browned. Using a slotted spoon, transfer to a plate.

3 Add the remaining olive oil to the saucepan, then add the onion and peppers. Reduce the heat to medium and cook, stirring frequently, until starting to colour and soften. Stir in the garlic and chorizo and continue to cook for a further 3 minutes. Add the rice and cook for about 2 minutes, stirring to coat with the oil, until the rice is translucent and golden.

4 Stir in the stock, crushed chillies, thyme, tomato purée and salt and pepper and bring to the boil. Return the chicken to the saucepan, pressing gently into the rice. Cover and cook over a very low heat for about 45 minutes until the chicken and rice are cooked and tender.

5 Gently stir in the ham, black olives and half the parsley. Cover and heat for a further 5 minutes. Sprinkle with the remaining parsley and serve immediately.

PAD THAI

INGREDIENTS   Serves 4

225 g/8 oz flat rice noodles

2 tbsp vegetable oil

225 g/8 oz boneless chicken breast, skinned and thinly sliced

4 shallots, peeled and thinly sliced

2 garlic cloves, peeled and finely chopped

4 spring onions, trimmed and diagonally cut into 5 cm/ 2 inch pieces

350 g/12 oz fresh white crab meat or tiny prawns

75 g/3 oz fresh bean sprouts, rinsed and drained

2 tbsp preserved or fresh radish, chopped

2–3 tbsp roasted peanuts, chopped (optional)

FOR THE SAUCE:

3 tbsp Thai fish sauce (nam pla)

2–3 tbsp rice vinegar or cider vinegar

1 tbsp chilli bean or oyster sauce

1 tbsp toasted sesame oil

1 tbsp light brown sugar

1 red chilli, deseeded and thinly sliced

1 To make the sauce, whisk all the sauce ingredients in a bowl and reserve. Put the rice noodles in a large bowl and pour over enough hot water to cover. Leave to stand for about 15 minutes until softened. Drain and rinse, then drain again.

2 Heat the oil in a wok over a high heat until hot, but not smoking. Add the chicken strips and stir-fry constantly until they begin to colour. Using a slotted spoon, transfer to a plate. Reduce the heat to medium-high.

3 Add the shallots, garlic and spring onions and stir-fry for 1 minute. Stir in the rice noodles, then the reserved sauce; mix well.

4 Add the reserved chicken strips, with the crab meat or prawns, bean sprouts and radish and stir well. Cook for about 5 minutes, stirring frequently, until heated through. If the noodles begin to stick, add a little water.

5 Turn into a large shallow serving dish and sprinkle with the chopped peanuts, if desired. Serve immediately.

HELPFUL HINT

Rice noodles are usually sold dried, but fresh noodles are sometimes available. Check packet instructions on use.

FRIED GINGER RICE WITH SOY GLAZED DUCK

INGREDIENTS   Serves 4–6

2 duck breasts, skinned and
  diagonally cut into thin slices
2–3 tbsp Japanese soy sauce
1 tbsp mirin (sweet rice wine)
  or sherry
2 tbsp brown sugar
5 cm/2 inch piece of fresh root
  ginger, peeled and finely
  chopped
4 tbsp peanut or vegetable oil
2 garlic cloves, peeled and
  crushed
300 g/11 oz long-grain brown
  rice

900 ml/1½ pints chicken stock
freshly ground black pepper
125 g/4 oz lean ham, diced
175 g/6 oz mangetout,
  diagonally cut in half
8 spring onions, trimmed and
  diagonally thinly sliced
1 tbsp freshly chopped
  coriander
sweet or hot chilli sauce, to
  taste (optional)
sprigs of fresh coriander, to
  garnish

1 Put the duck slices in a bowl with 1 tablespoon of the soy sauce, the mirin, 1 teaspoon of the sugar and one-third of the ginger; stir. Leave to stand.

2 Heat 2 tablespoons of the oil in a large heavy-based saucepan. Add the garlic and half the remaining ginger and stir-fry for 1 minute. Add the rice and cook for 3 minutes, stirring constantly, until translucent.

3 Stir in all but 125 ml/4 fl oz of the stock, with 1 teaspoon of the soy sauce, and bring to the boil. Season with pepper. Reduce the heat to very low and simmer, covered, for 25–30 minutes until the rice is tender and the liquid is absorbed. Cover and leave to stand.

4 Heat the remaining oil in a large frying pan or wok. Drain the duck strips and add to the frying pan. Stir-fry for 2–3 minutes until just coloured. Add 1 tablespoon of soy sauce and the remaining sugar and cook for 1 minute until glazed. Transfer to a plate and keep warm.

5 Stir in the ham, mangetout, spring onions, the remaining ginger and the chopped coriander. Add the remaining stock and duck marinade and cook until the liquid is almost reduced. Fork in the rice and a little chilli sauce to taste (if using); stir well. Turn into a serving dish and top with the duck. Garnish with coriander sprigs and serve immediately.

PERSIAN CHICKEN PILAF

INGREDIENTS

Serves 4–6

2–3 tbsp vegetable oil
700 g/1½ lb boneless skinless
  chicken pieces (breast and
  thighs), cut into 2.5 cm/
  1 inch pieces
2 medium onions, peeled and
  coarsely chopped
1 tsp ground cumin
200 g/7 oz long-grain white
  rice
1 tbsp tomato purée
1 tsp saffron strands

salt and freshly ground black
  pepper
100 ml/3½ fl oz pomegranate
  juice
900 ml/1½ pints chicken stock
125 g/4 oz ready-to-eat dried
  apricots or prunes, halved
2 tbsp raisins
2 tbsp freshly chopped mint or
  parsley
pomegranate seeds, to
  garnish (optional)

1 Heat the oil in a large heavy-based saucepan over a medium-high heat. Cook the chicken pieces, in batches, until lightly browned. Return all the browned chicken to the saucepan.

2 Add the onions to the saucepan, reduce the heat to medium and cook for 3–5 minutes, stirring frequently, until the onions begin to soften. Add the cumin and rice and stir to coat the rice. Cook for about 2 minutes until the rice is golden and translucent. Stir in the tomato purée and the saffron strands, then season to taste with salt and pepper.

3 Add the pomegranate juice and stock and bring to the boil, stirring once or twice. Add the apricots or prunes and raisins and stir gently. Reduce the heat to low and cook for 30 minutes until the chicken and rice are tender and the liquid is absorbed.

4 Turn into a shallow serving dish and sprinkle with the chopped mint or parsley. Serve immediately, garnished with pomegranate seeds, if using.

HELPFUL HINT

Pomegranate juice is available from Middle Eastern groceries and some specialty shops. You can extract juice from fresh pomegranates by separating the seeds from the bitter pith and membranes, then crushing the seeds in a sieve placed over a bowl. Substitute unsweetened grape or apple juice if you can not get pomegranates.

CHICKEN & SEAFOOD RISOTTO

INGREDIENTS   Serves 6–8

125 ml/4 fl oz olive oil

1.4 kg/3 lb chicken, cut into
 8 pieces

350 g/12 oz spicy chorizo
 sausage, cut into 1 cm/½ inch
 pieces

125 g/4 oz cured ham, diced

1 onion, peeled and chopped

2 red or yellow peppers,
 deseeded and cut into
 2.5 cm/1 inch pieces

4 garlic cloves, peeled and
 finely chopped

750 g/1 lb 10 oz short-grain
 Spanish rice or Arborio rice

2 bay leaves

1 tsp dried thyme

1 tsp saffron strands, lightly
 crushed

200 ml/7 fl oz dry white wine

1.6 litres/2¾ pints chicken stock

salt and freshly ground black
 pepper

125 g/4 oz fresh shelled peas

450 g/1 lb uncooked prawns

36 clams and/or mussels, well
 scrubbed

2 tbsp freshly chopped parsley

TO GARNISH:

lemon wedges

fresh parsley sprigs

1 Heat half the oil in a 45.5 cm/18 inch paella pan or deep wide frying pan. Add the chicken pieces and fry for 15 minutes, turning constantly, until golden. Remove from the pan and reserve. Add the chorizo and ham to the pan and cook for 6 minutes until crisp, stirring occasionally. Remove and add to the chicken.

2 Add the onion to the pan and cook for 3 minutes, or until beginning to soften. Add the peppers and garlic and cook for 2 minutes; add to the reserved chicken, chorizo and ham.

3 Add the remaining oil to the pan and stir in the rice until well coated. Stir in the bay leaves, thyme and saffron, then pour in

the wine and bubble until evaporated, stirring and scraping up any bits on the bottom of the pan. Stir in the stock and bring to the boil, stirring occasionally.

4 Return the chicken, chorizo, ham and vegetables to the pan, burying them gently in the rice. Season to taste with salt and pepper. Reduce the heat and simmer for 10 minutes, stirring occasionally.

5 Add the peas and seafood, pushing them gently into the rice. Cover, cook over a low heat for 5 minutes, or until the rice and prawns are tender and the clams and mussels open (discard any that do not open). Stand for 5 minutes. Sprinkle with the parsley, garnish and serve.

NEW ORLEANS JAMBALAYA

INGREDIENTS   Serves 6–8

FOR THE SEASONING MIX:
2 dried bay leaves
1 tsp salt
2 tsp cayenne pepper, or to taste
2 tsp dried oregano
1 tsp each ground white and black pepper, or to taste

3 tbsp vegetable oil
125 g/4 oz ham
225 g/8 oz smoked pork sausage, cut into chunks
2 large onions, peeled and chopped

4 celery stalks, trimmed and chopped
2 green peppers, deseeded and chopped
2 garlic cloves, peeled and finely chopped
350 g/12 oz raw chicken, diced
400 g can chopped tomatoes
600 ml/1 pint fish stock
400 g/14 oz long-grain white rice
4 spring onions, trimmed and coarsely chopped
275 g/10 oz raw prawns, peeled
250 g/9 oz white crab meat

1 Mix all the seasoning ingredients together in a small bowl and reserve.

2 Heat 2 tablespoons of the oil in a large flameproof casserole over a medium heat. Add the ham and sausage and cook, stirring often, for 7–8 minutes until golden. Remove from the pan and reserve.

3 Add the remaining onions, celery and peppers to the casserole and cook for about 4 minutes, or until softened, stirring occasionally. Stir in the garlic, then using a slotted spoon, transfer all the vegetables to a plate and reserve with the sausage.

4 Add the chicken pieces to the casserole and cook for about 4 minutes, or until beginning to colour, turning once. Stir in the seasoning mix and turn the pieces to coat well. Return the sausage and vegetables to the casserole and stir well. Add the chopped tomatoes, with their juice, and the stock and bring to the boil.

5 Stir in the rice and reduce the heat to low. Cover and simmer for 12 minutes. Uncover, stir in the spring onions and prawns and cook, covered, for a further 4 minutes. Add the crab and gently stir in. Cook for 2–3 minutes, or until the rice is tender. Remove from the heat, cover and leave to stand for 5 minutes before serving.

FRUITY RICE-STUFFED POUSSINS

INGREDIENTS   Serves 6

FOR THE RICE STUFFING:
225 ml/8 fl oz port
125 g/4 oz raisins
125 g/4 oz ready-to-eat dried
   apricots, chopped
2 tbsp olive oil
1 medium onion, peeled and
   finely chopped
1 celery stalk, trimmed and
   finely sliced
2 garlic cloves, peeled and
   finely chopped
1½ tsp mixed spice
1 tsp each dried oregano and
   mint or basil
225 g/8 oz unsweetened
   canned chestnuts, chopped
200 g/7 oz long-grain white
   rice, cooked

grated rind and juice of 2
   oranges
350 ml/12 fl oz chicken stock
50 g/2 oz walnut halves, lightly
   toasted and chopped
2 tbsp each freshly chopped
   mint and parsley
salt and freshly ground black
   pepper

6 oven-ready poussins
50 g/2 oz butter, melted

TO GARNISH:
fresh herbs
orange wedges

1 Preheat the oven to 180°C/ 350°F/Gas Mark 4. To make the stuffing, place the port, raisins and apricots in a bowl and leave for 15 minutes. Heat the oil in a large saucepan. Add the onion and celery and cook for 3–4 minutes. Add the garlic, mixed spice, herbs and chestnuts and cook for 4 minutes, stirring occasionally. Add the rice, half the orange rind and juice and the stock. Simmer for 5 minutes until most liquid is absorbed.

2 Drain the raisins and apricots, reserving the port. Stir into the rice with the walnuts, mint, parsley and seasoning and cook for 2 minutes. Remove and cool.

3 Rinse the poussin cavities, pat dry and season with salt and pepper. Lightly fill the cavities with the stuffing. Tie the legs of together, tucking in the tail. Form any extra stuffing into balls.

4 Place in roasting tins with stuffing balls and brush with melted butter. Drizzle over the remaining butter, remaining orange rind and juice and port. Roast in the preheated oven for 50 minutes or until golden and cooked, basting every 15 minutes. Transfer to a platter, cover with tinfoil and rest. Pour over any pan juices. Garnish with herbs and orange wedges. Serve with the stuffing.

CREAMY CHICKEN & RICE PILAU

INGREDIENTS   Serves 4–6

350 g/12 oz basmati rice
salt and freshly ground black
  pepper
50 g/2 oz butter
100 g/3½ oz flaked almonds
75 g/3 oz unsalted shelled
  pistachio nuts
4–6 skinless chicken breast
  fillets, each cut into 4 pieces
2 tbsp vegetable oil
2 medium onions, peeled and
  thinly sliced
2 garlic cloves, peeled and
  finely chopped
2.5 cm/1 inch piece of fresh

root ginger, finely chopped
6 green cardamom pods,
  lightly crushed
4–6 whole cloves
2 bay leaves
1 tsp ground coriander
½ tsp cayenne pepper, or to
  taste
225 ml/8 fl oz natural yogurt
225 ml/8 fl oz double cream
225 g/8 oz seedless green
  grapes, halved if large
2 tbsp freshly chopped
  coriander or mint

1 Bring a saucepan of lightly salted water to the boil. Gradually pour in the rice; return to the boil, then simmer for about 12 minutes until tender. Drain, rinse under cold water and reserve.

2 Heat the butter in a large deep frying pan over a medium-high heat. Add the almonds and pistachios and cook for about 2 minutes, stirring constantly, until golden. Using a slotted spoon, transfer to a plate.

3 Add the chicken pieces to the pan and cook for 5 minutes, or until golden, turning once. Remove from the pan and reserve. Add the oil to the pan and cook the onions for 10 minutes, or

until golden, stirring frequently. Stir in the garlic, ginger and spices and cook for 2–3 minutes, stirring.

4 Add 2–3 tablespoons of the yogurt and cook, stirring until the moisture evaporates. Continue adding the yogurt in this way until it is used up.

5 Return the chicken and nuts to the pan and stir. Stir in 125 ml/4 fl oz of boiling water and season to taste with salt and pepper. Cook, covered, over a low heat for 10 minutes until the chicken is tender. Stir in the cream, grapes and half the herbs. Gently fold in the rice. Heat through for 5 minutes and sprinkle with the remaining herbs, then serve.

WILD RICE & BACON SALAD WITH SMOKED CHICKEN

INGREDIENTS   Serves 4

150 g/5 oz wild rice
50 g/2 oz pecan or walnut
  halves
1 tbsp vegetable oil
4 slices smoked bacon, diced
3–4 shallots, peeled and finely
  chopped
75 ml/3 fl oz walnut oil

2–3 tbsp sherry or cider
  vinegar
2 tbsp freshly chopped dill
salt and freshly ground black
  pepper
275 g/10 oz smoked chicken or
  duck breast, thinly sliced
dill sprigs, to garnish

1 Put the wild rice in a medium saucepan with 600 ml/1 pint water and bring to the boil, stirring once or twice. Reduce the heat, cover and simmer gently for 30–50 minutes, depending on the texture you prefer, chewy or tender. Using a fork, gently fluff into a large bowl and leave to cool slightly.

2 Meanwhile, toast the nuts in a frying pan over a medium heat for 2 minutes, or until they are fragrant and lightly coloured, stirring and tossing frequently. Cool, then chop coarsely and add to the rice.

3 Heat the oil in the frying pan over a medium heat. Add the bacon and cook, stirring from time to time, for 3–4 minutes, or until crisp and brown. Remove from the pan and drain on absorbent kitchen paper. Add the shallots to the pan and cook for 4 minutes, or until just softened, stirring

from time to time. Stir into the rice and nuts, with the drained bacon pieces.

4 Whisk the walnut oil, vinegar, half the dill and salt and pepper in a small bowl until combined. Pour the dressing over the rice mixture and toss well to combine. Mix the chicken and the remaining chopped dill into the rice, then spoon into bowls and garnish each serving with a dill sprig. Serve slightly warm, or at room temperature.

FOOD FACT

Both smoked chicken and duck have a delicate smoky flavour which comes from being first cold-smoked, then briefly hot-smoked. You can, of course, use plain roasted chicken or duck if you prefer.

CHICKEN & WHITE WINE RISOTTO

INGREDIENTS   Serves 4–6

2 tbsp oil
125 g/4 oz unsalted butter
2 shallots, peeled and finely
    chopped
300 g/11 oz Arborio rice
600 ml/1 pint dry white wine
750 ml/1¼ pints chicken stock,
    heated
350 g/12 oz skinless chicken
    breast fillets, thinly sliced

50 g/2 oz Parmesan cheese,
    grated
2 tbsp freshly chopped dill or
    parsley
salt and freshly ground black
    pepper

1 Heat the oil and half the
butter in a large heavy-based
saucepan over a medium-high
heat. Add the shallots and cook
for 2 minutes, or until softened,
stirring frequently. Add the rice
and cook for 2–3 minutes,
stirring frequently, until the rice
is translucent and well coated.

2 Pour in half the wine; it will
bubble and steam rapidly.
Cook, stirring constantly, until
the liquid is absorbed. Add a
ladleful of the hot stock and cook
until the liquid is absorbed.
Carefully stir in the chicken.

3 Continue adding the stock,
about half a ladleful at a
time, allowing each addition to
be absorbed before adding the
next; never allow the rice to cook
dry. This process should take
about 20 minutes. The risotto
should have a creamy consistency
and the rice should be tender, but
firm to the bite.

4 Stir in the remaining wine
and cook for 2–3 minutes.
Remove from the heat and stir
in the remaining butter with
the Parmesan cheese and half
the chopped herbs. Season
to taste with salt and pepper.
Spoon into warmed shallow
bowls and sprinkle each with
the remaining chopped herbs.
Serve immediately.

HELPFUL HINT

Keep the stock to be added to
the risotto at a low simmer in
a separate saucepan, so that
it is piping hot when added to
the rice. This will ensure that
the dish is kept at a constant
heat during cooking, which is
important to achieve a perfect
creamy texture.

POTATO-STUFFED ROAST POUSSIN

INGREDIENTS   Serves 4

4 oven-ready poussins
salt and freshly ground black
   pepper
1 lemon, cut into quarters
450 g/1 lb floury potatoes,
   peeled and cut into 4 cm/
   1½ inch pieces
1 tbsp freshly chopped thyme
   or rosemary
3–4 tbsp olive oil

4 garlic cloves, unpeeled and
   lightly smashed
8 slices streaky bacon or
   Parma ham
125 ml/4 fl oz white wine
2 spring onions, trimmed and
   thinly sliced
2 tbsp double cream or crème
   fraîche
lemon wedges, to garnish

1 Preheat the oven to 220°C/
425°F/Gas Mark 7. Place a
roasting tin in the oven to heat.
Rinse the poussin cavities and
pat dry with absorbent kitchen
paper. Season the cavities with
salt and pepper and a squeeze of
lemon. Push a lemon quarter
into each cavity.

2 Put the potatoes in a
saucepan of lightly salted
water and bring to the boil.
Reduce the heat to low and
simmer until just tender; do not
overcook. Drain and cool slightly.
Sprinkle the chopped herbs over
the potatoes and drizzle with 2–3
tablespoons of the oil.

3 Spoon half the seasoned
potatoes into the poussin
cavities; do not pack too tightly.
Rub each poussin with a little
more oil and season with pepper.
Carefully spoon 1 tablespoon of
oil into the hot roasting tin and
arrange the poussins in the tin.

Spoon the remaining potatoes
around the edge. Sprinkle over
the garlic.

4 Roast the poussins in the
preheated oven for 30
minutes, or until the skin is
golden and beginning to crisp.
Carefully lay the bacon slices over
the breast of each poussin and
continue to roast for 15–20
minutes until crisp and the
poussins are cooked through.

5 Transfer the poussins
and potatoes to a serving
platter and cover loosely with
tinfoil. Skim off the fat from
the juices. Place the tin over a
medium heat, add the wine
and spring onions. Cook briefly,
scraping the bits from the bottom
of the tin. Whisk in the cream
or crème fraîche and bubble for
1 minute, or until thickened.
Garnish the poussins with
lemon wedges, and serve
with the creamy gravy.

TURKEY HASH WITH POTATO & BEETROOT

INGREDIENTS   Serves 4–6

2 tbsp vegetable oil
50 g/2 oz butter
4 slices streaky bacon, diced
  or sliced
1 medium onion, peeled and
  finely chopped
450 g/1 lb cooked turkey, diced

450 g/1 lb finely chopped
  cooked potatoes
2–3 tbsp freshly chopped
  parsley
2 tbsp plain flour
250 g/9 oz cooked medium
  beetroot, diced
green salad, to serve

1 In a large, heavy-based frying pan, heat the oil and half the butter over a medium heat until sizzling. Add the bacon and cook for 4 minutes, or until crisp and golden, stirring occasionally. Using a slotted spoon, transfer to a large bowl. Add the onion to the pan and cook for 3–4 minutes, or until soft and golden, stirring frequently.

2 Meanwhile, add the turkey, potatoes, parsley and flour to the cooked bacon in the bowl. Stir and toss gently, then fold in the diced beetroot.

3 Add half the remaining butter to the frying pan and then the turkey vegetable mixture. Stir, then spread the mixture to evenly cover the bottom of the frying pan. Cook for 15 minutes, or until the underside is crisp and brown, pressing the hash firmly into a cake with a spatula. Remove from the heat.

4 Invert a large plate over the frying pan and, holding the plate and frying pan together with an oven glove, turn the hash out onto the plate. Heat the remaining butter in the pan, slide the hash back into the pan and cook for 4 minutes, or until crisp and brown on the other side. Invert onto the plate again and serve immediately with a green salad.

TASTY TIP

A hash is usually made just with potatoes, but here they are combined with ruby red beetroot, which adds vibrant colour and a sweet earthy flavour to the dish. Make sure that you buy plainly cooked beetroot, rather than the type preserved in vinegar.

CHICKEN & NEW POTATOES ON ROSEMARY SKEWERS

INGREDIENTS   Serves 4

8 thick fresh rosemary stems,
  at least 23 cm/9 inches long
3–4 tbsp extra-virgin olive oil
2 garlic cloves, peeled and
  crushed
1 tsp freshly chopped thyme
grated rind and juice of 1
  lemon
salt and freshly ground black
  pepper

4 skinless chicken breast fillets
16 small new potatoes, peeled
  or scrubbed
8 very small onions or
  shallots, peeled
1 large yellow or red pepper,
  deseeded
lemon wedges, to garnish
parsley-flavoured cooked rice,
  to serve

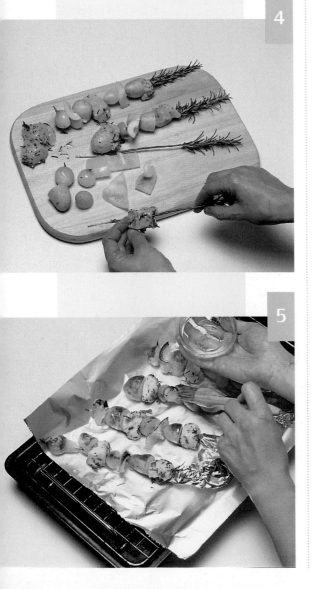

1 Preheat the grill and line the grill rack with tinfoil just before cooking. If using a barbecue, light at least 20 minutes before required. Strip the leaves from the rosemary stems, leaving about 5 cm/2 inches of soft leaves at the top. Chop the leaves coarsely and reserve. Using a sharp knife, cut the thicker woody ends of the stems to a point which can pierce the chicken pieces and potatoes. Blend the chopped rosemary, oil, garlic, thyme and lemon rind and juice in a shallow dish. Season to taste with salt and pepper.

2 Cut the chicken into 4 cm/ ½ inch cubes, add to the flavoured oil and stir well. Cover, refrigerate for at least 30 minutes, turning occasionally.

3 Cook the potatoes in lightly salted boiling water for 10–12 minutes until just tender.

Add the onions to the potatoes 2 minutes before the end of the cooking time. Drain, rinse under cold running water and leave to cool. Cut the pepper into 2.5 cm/ 1 inch squares.

4 Beginning with a piece of chicken and starting with the pointed end of the skewer, alternately thread equal amounts of chicken, potato, pepper and onion onto each rosemary skewer. Cover the leafy ends of the skewers with tinfoil to stop them from burning. Do not thread the chicken and vegetables too closely together on the skewer or the chicken may not cook completely.

5 Cook the kebabs for 15 minutes, or until tender and golden, turning and brushing with either extra oil or the marinade. Remove the tinfoil, garnish with lemon wedges and serve on rice.

AROMATIC DUCK BURGERS ON POTATO PANCAKES

INGREDIENTS   Serves 4

700 g/1½ lb boneless duck
  breasts
2 tbsp hoisin sauce
1 garlic clove, peeled and
  finely chopped
4 spring onions, trimmed and
  finely chopped
2 tbsp Japanese soy sauce
½ tsp Chinese five-spice powder
salt and freshly ground black
  pepper

freshly chopped coriander, to
  garnish
extra hoisin sauce, to serve

FOR THE POTATO PANCAKES:
450 g/1 lb floury potatoes
1 small onion, peeled and
  grated
1 small egg, beaten
1 heaped tbsp plain flour

1 Peel off the thick layer of fat from the duck breasts and cut into small pieces. Put the fat in a small dry saucepan and set over a low heat for 10–15 minutes, or until the fat runs clear and the crackling goes crisp; reserve.

2 Cut the duck meat into pieces and blend in a food processor until coarsely chopped. Spoon into a bowl and add the hoisin sauce, garlic, half the spring onions, soy sauce and Chinese five-spice powder. Season to taste with salt and pepper and shape into 4 burgers. Cover and chill in the refrigerator for 1 hour.

3 To make the potato pancakes, grate the potatoes into a large bowl, squeeze out the water with your hands, then put on a clean tea towel and twist the ends to squeeze out any remaining water.

Return the potato to the bowl, add the onion and egg and mix well. Add the flour and salt and pepper. Stir to blend.

4 Heat about 2 tablespoons of the clear duck fat in a large frying pan. Spoon the potato mixture into 2–4 pattie shapes and cook for 6 minutes, or until golden and crisp, turning once. Keep warm in the oven. Repeat with the remaining mixture, adding duck fat as needed.

5 Preheat the grill and line the grill rack with tinfoil. Brush the burgers with a little of the duck fat and grill for 6–8 minutes, or longer if wished, turning once. Arrange 1–2 potato pancakes on a plate and top with a burger. Spoon over a little hoisin sauce and garnish with the remaining spring onions and coriander.

CHICKEN PIE WITH SWEET POTATO TOPPING

INGREDIENTS   Serves 4

700 g/1½ lb sweet potatoes,
    peeled and cut into chunks
salt and freshly ground black
    pepper
250 g/9 oz potatoes, peeled
    and cut into chunks
150 ml/¼ pint milk
25 g/1 oz butter
2 tsp brown sugar
grated rind of 1 orange
4 skinless chicken breast
    fillets, diced

1 medium onion, peeled and
    coarsely chopped
125 g/4 oz baby mushrooms,
    stems trimmed
2 leeks, trimmed and thickly
    sliced
150 ml/¼ pint dry white wine
1 chicken stock cube
1 tbsp freshly chopped parsley
50 ml/2 fl oz crème fraîche or
    thick double cream
green vegetables, to serve

1 Preheat the oven to 190°C/
375°F/Gas Mark 5, 10
minutes before required. Cook
the potatoes in lightly salted
boiling water until tender. Drain
well, then return to the saucepan
and mash until smooth and
creamy, gradually adding the
milk, then the butter, sugar and
orange rind. Season to taste with
salt and pepper and reserve.

2 Place the chicken in a
saucepan with the onion,
mushrooms, leeks, wine, stock
cube and season to taste. Simmer,
covered, until the chicken and
vegetables are tender. Using a
slotted spoon, transfer the
chicken and vegetables to a
1.1 litre/2 pint pie dish. Add the
parsley and crème fraîche or
cream to the liquid in the pan and
bring to the boil. Simmer until

thickened and smooth, stirring
constantly. Pour over the chicken
in the pie dish, mix and cool.

3 Spread the mashed potato
over the chicken filling, and
swirl the surface into decorative
peaks. Bake in the preheated oven
for 35 minutes, or until the top is
golden and the chicken filling is
heated through. Serve immediately
with fresh green vegetables.

HELPFUL HINT

There are 2 types of sweet
potato; one has a creamy-
coloured flesh, the other
orange. Both are suitable for
mashing as in this recipe, but
the cream-coloured variety
has a drier texture, so you
may need a little more milk.

WARM CHICKEN & POTATO SALAD WITH PEAS & MINT

INGREDIENTS

Serves 4–6

450 g/1 lb new potatoes, peeled or scrubbed and cut into bite-sized pieces
salt and freshly ground black pepper
2 tbsp cider vinegar
175 g/6 oz frozen garden peas, thawed
1 small ripe avocado
4 cooked chicken breasts, about 450 g/1 lb in weight, skinned and diced

2 tbsp freshly chopped mint
2 heads Little Gem lettuce
fresh mint sprigs, to garnish

FOR THE DRESSING:
2 tbsp raspberry or sherry vinegar
2 tsp Dijon mustard
1 tsp clear honey
50 ml/2 fl oz sunflower oil
50 ml/2 fl oz extra-virgin olive oil

1 Cook the potatoes in lightly salted boiling water for 15 minutes, or until just tender when pierced with the tip of a sharp knife; do not overcook. Rinse under cold running water to cool slightly, then drain and turn into a large bowl. Sprinkle with the cider vinegar and toss gently.

2 Run the peas under hot water to ensure that they are thawed, pat dry with absorbent kitchen paper and add to the potatoes.

3 Cut the avocado in half lengthways and remove the stone. Peel and cut the avocado into cubes and add to the potatoes and peas. Add the chicken and stir together lightly.

4 To make the dressing, place all the ingredients in a screw-top jar, with a little salt and pepper and shake well to mix; add a little more oil if the flavour is too sharp. Pour over the salad and toss gently to coat. Sprinkle in half the mint and stir lightly.

5 Separate the lettuce leaves and spread onto a large shallow serving plate. Spoon the salad on top and sprinkle with the remaining mint. Garnish with mint sprigs and serve.

FOOD FACT

Cider vinegar, made from cider as its name suggests, has a strong sharp flavour with a hint of apples. Raspberry vinegar has a wine vinegar base, macerated with fresh raspberries.

BROWN RICE & LENTIL SALAD WITH DUCK

INGREDIENTS   Serves 6

225 g/8 oz Puy lentils, rinsed
4 tbsp olive oil
1 medium onion, peeled and
  finely chopped
200 g/7 oz long-grain brown
  rice
½ tsp dried thyme
450 ml/¾ pint chicken stock
salt and freshly ground black
  pepper
350 g/12 oz shiitake or
  portabella mushrooms,
  trimmed and sliced
375 g/13 oz cooked Chinese-
  style spicy duck or roasted
  duck, sliced into chunks
2 garlic cloves, peeled and
  finely chopped

125 g/4 oz cooked smoked
  ham, diced
2 small courgettes, trimmed,
  diced and blanched
6 spring onions, trimmed and
  thinly sliced
2 tbsp freshly chopped parsley
2 tbsp walnut halves, toasted
  and chopped

FOR THE DRESSING:

2 tbsp red or white wine vinegar
1 tbsp balsamic vinegar
1 tsp Dijon mustard
1 tsp clear honey
75 ml/3 fl oz extra-virgin olive
  oil
2–3 tbsp walnut oil

1 Bring a large saucepan of water to the boil, sprinkle in the lentils, return to the boil, then simmer over a low heat for 30 minutes, or until tender; do not overcook. Drain and rinse under cold running water, then drain again and reserve.

2 Heat 2 tablespoons of the oil in a saucepan. Add the onion and cook for 2 minutes until it begins to soften. Stir in the rice with the thyme and stock. Season to taste with salt and pepper and bring to the boil. Cover and simmer for 40 minutes, or until tender and the liquid is absorbed.

3 Heat the remaining oil in a large frying pan and add the mushrooms. Cook for 5 minutes until golden. Stir in the duck and garlic and cook for 2–3 minutes to heat through. Season well.

4 To make the dressing, whisk the vinegars, mustard and honey in a large serving bowl, then gradually whisk in the oils. Add the lentils and the rice, then stir lightly together. Gently stir in the ham, blanched courgettes, spring onions and parsley. Season to taste and sprinkle with the walnuts. Serve topped with the duck and mushrooms.

CHINESE-STYLE FRIED RICE

INGREDIENTS

Serves 4–6

2–3 tbsp groundnut oil or vegetable oil

2 small onions, peeled and cut into wedges

2 garlic cloves, peeled and thinly sliced

2.5 cm/1 inch piece of fresh root ginger, peeled and cut into thin slivers

225 g/8 oz cooked chicken, thinly sliced

125 g/4 oz cooked ham, thinly sliced

350 g/12 oz cooked cold long-grain white rice

125 g/4 oz canned water chestnuts, sliced

225 g/8 oz cooked peeled prawns (optional)

3 large eggs

3 tsp sesame oil

salt and freshly ground black pepper

6 spring onions, trimmed and sliced into 1 cm/½ inch pieces

2 tbsp dark soy sauce

1 tbsp sweet chilli sauce

2 tbsp freshly chopped coriander

TO GARNISH:

2 tbsp chopped roasted peanuts

sprig of fresh coriander

1 Heat a wok or large deep frying pan until very hot, add the oil and heat for 30 seconds. Add the onions and stir-fry for 2 minutes. Stir in the garlic and ginger and cook for 1 minute. Add the cooked sliced chicken and ham and stir-fry for a further 2–3 minutes.

2 Add the rice, the water chestnuts and prawns, if using, with 2 tablespoons of water, and stir-fry for 2 minutes until the rice is heated through.

3 Beat the eggs with 1 teaspoon of the sesame oil and season to taste with salt and pepper. Make a well in the centre of the rice, then pour in the egg mixture and stir immediately, gradually drawing the rice mixture into the egg, until the egg is cooked.

4 Add the spring onions, soy and chilli sauces, coriander and a little water, if necessary. Adjust the seasoning and drizzle with the remaining sesame oil. Sprinkle with the nuts and serve.

HELPFUL HINT

Long-grain white rice absorbs about 3 times its weight during cooking, so if cooking rice specially for this dish you will need 225 g/8 oz raw rice. Add extra flavour by cooking in vegetable or chicken stock.

TURKEY & PESTO RICE ROULADES

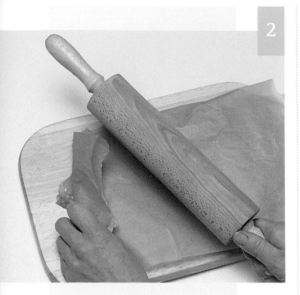

INGREDIENTS   Serves 4

125 g/4 oz cooked white rice,
   at room temperature
1 garlic clove, peeled and
   crushed
1–2 tbsp Parmesan cheese,
   grated
2 tbsp prepared pesto sauce
2 tbsp pine nuts, lightly
   toasted and chopped
4 turkey steaks, each weighing
   about 150 g/5 oz

salt and freshly ground black
   pepper
4 slices Parma ham
2 tbsp olive oil
50 ml/2 fl oz white wine
25 g/1 oz unsalted butter,
   chilled

TO SERVE:
freshly cooked spinach
freshly cooked pasta

1 Put the rice in a bowl and add the garlic, Parmesan cheese, pesto and pine nuts. Stir to combine the ingredients, then reserve.

2 Place the turkey steaks on a chopping board and, using a sharp knife, cut horizontally through each steak, without cutting right through. Open up the steaks and cover with baking parchment. Flatten slightly by pounding with a meat mallet or rolling pin.

3 Season each steak with salt and pepper. Divide the stuffing equally among the steaks, spreading evenly over one half. Fold the steaks in half to enclose the filling, then wrap each steak in a slice of Parma ham and secure with cocktail sticks.

4 Heat the oil in a large frying pan over medium heat. Cook the steaks for 5 minutes, or until golden on one side. Turn and cook for a further 2 minutes. Push the steaks to the side and pour in the wine. Allow the wine to bubble and evaporate. Add the butter, a little at a time, whisking constantly until the sauce is smooth. Discard the cocktail sticks, then serve the steaks drizzled with the sauce and serve with spinach and pasta.

FOOD FACT

The classic Italian Parma ham is dry-cured, whereby it is rubbed with salt for about a month, then hung up to dry for a year. Carved very thinly, it often served raw, but is also good when lightly fried.

SLOW ROAST CHICKEN WITH POTATOES & OREGANO

INGREDIENTS   Serves 6

1.4–1.8 kg/3–4 lb oven-ready
  chicken, preferably free
  range
1 lemon, halved
1 onion, peeled and quartered
50 g/2 oz butter, softened
salt and freshly ground black
  pepper

1 kg/2¼ lb potatoes, peeled
  and quartered
3–4 tbsp extra-virgin olive oil
1 tbsp dried oregano,
  crumbled
1 tsp fresh thyme leaves
2 tbsp freshly chopped thyme
fresh sage leaves, to garnish

1 Preheat the oven to 200°C/ 400°F/Gas Mark 6. Rinse the chicken and dry well, inside and out, with absorbent kitchen paper. Rub the chicken all over with the lemon halves, then squeeze the juice over it and into the cavity. Put the squeezed halves into the cavity with the quartered onion.

2 Rub the softened butter all over the chicken and season to taste with salt and pepper, then put it in a large roasting tin, breast-side down.

3 Toss the potatoes in the oil, season with salt and pepper to taste and add the dried oregano and fresh thyme. Arrange the potatoes with the oil around the chicken and carefully pour 150 ml/¼ pint water into one end of the pan (not over the oil).

4 Roast in the preheated oven for 25 minutes. Reduce the oven temperature to 190°C/

375°F/Gas Mark 5 and turn the chicken breast-side up. Turn the potatoes, sprinkle over half the fresh herbs and baste the chicken and potatoes with the juices. Continue roasting for 1 hour, or until the chicken is cooked, basting occasionally. If the liquid evaporates completely, add a little more water. The chicken is done when the juices run clear when the thigh is pierced with a skewer.

5 Transfer the chicken to a carving board and rest for 5 minutes, covered with tinfoil. Return the potatoes to the oven while the chicken is resting.

6 Carve the chicken into serving pieces and arrange on a large heatproof serving dish. Arrange the potatoes around the chicken and drizzle over any remaining juices. Sprinkle with the remaining herbs and serve.

LEEK & POTATO TART

INGREDIENTS   Serves 6

225 g/8 oz plain flour
pinch of salt
150 g/5 oz butter, cubed
50 g/2 oz walnuts, very finely
  chopped
1 large egg yolk

FOR THE FILLING:
450 g/1 lb leeks, trimmed and
  thinly sliced
40 g/1½ oz butter

450 g/1 lb large new potatoes,
  scrubbed
300 ml/½ pint soured cream
3 medium eggs, lightly beaten
175 g/6 oz Gruyère cheese,
  grated
freshly grated nutmeg
salt and freshly ground black
  pepper
fresh chives, to garnish

1 Preheat the oven to 200°C/400°F/Gas Mark 6, about 15 minutes before baking. Sift the flour and salt into a bowl. Rub in the butter until the mixture resembles breadcrumbs. Stir in the nuts. Mix together the egg yolk and 3 tablespoons of cold water. Sprinkle over the dry ingredients. Mix to form a dough.

2 Knead on a lightly floured surface for a few seconds, then wrap in clingfilm and chill in the refrigerator for 20 minutes. Roll out and use to line a 20.5 cm/8 inch spring-form tin or very deep flan tin. Chill for a further 30 minutes.

3 Cook the leeks in the butter over a high heat for 2–3 minutes, stirring constantly. Lower the heat, cover and cook for 25 minutes until soft, stirring occasionally. Remove the leeks from the heat.

4 Cook the potatoes in boiling salted water for 15 minutes, or until almost tender. Drain and thickly slice. Add to the leeks. Stir the soured cream into the leeks and potatoes, followed by the eggs, cheese, nutmeg and salt and pepper. Pour into the pastry case and bake on the middle shelf in the preheated oven for 20 minutes.

5 Reduce the oven temperature to 190°C/375°F/Gas Mark 5 and cook for a further 30–35 minutes, or until the filling is set. Garnish with chives and serve immediately.

TASTY TIP

To ring the changes, flavour the pastry with different nuts, such as hazelnuts or almonds, or replace the nuts with 3 tablespoons of freshly chopped mixed herbs.

POTATO GNOCCHI WITH PESTO SAUCE

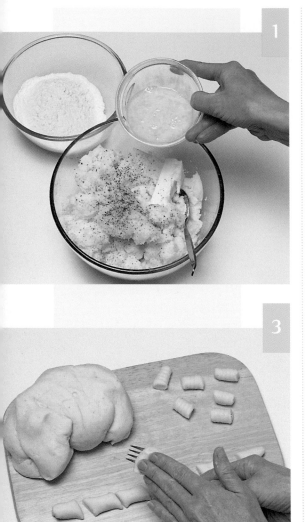

INGREDIENTS   Serves 6

900 g/2 lb floury potatoes
40 g/1½ oz butter
1 medium egg, beaten
225 g/8 oz plain flour
1 tsp salt
freshly ground black pepper
25 g/1 oz Parmesan cheese,
  shaved
rocket salad, to serve

FOR THE PESTO SAUCE:
50 g/2 oz fresh basil leaves
1 large garlic clove, peeled
2 tbsp pine nuts
125 ml/4 fl oz olive oil
40 g/1½ oz Parmesan cheese,
  grated

1 Cook the potatoes in their skins in boiling water for 20 minutes, or until tender. Drain and peel. While still warm, push the potatoes through a fine sieve into a bowl. Stir in the butter, egg, 175 g/6 oz of the flour, the salt and pepper.

2 Sift the remaining flour onto a board or work surface, add the potato mixture. Gently knead in enough flour until a soft, slightly sticky dough is formed.

3 With floured hands, break off portions of the dough and roll into 2.5 cm/1 inch thick ropes. Cut into 2 cm/¾ inch lengths. Lightly press each piece against the inner prongs of a fork. Put on a tray covered with a floured tea towel and chill in the refrigerator for about 30 minutes.

4 To make the pesto sauce, put the basil, garlic, pine nuts

and oil in a processor and blend until smooth and creamy. Turn into a bowl and stir in the Parmesan cheese. Season to taste.

5 Cooking in several batches, drop the gnocchi into a saucepan of barely simmering salted water. Cook for 3–4 minutes, or until they float to the surface. Remove with a slotted spoon and keep warm in a covered oiled baking dish in a low oven.

6 Add the gnocchi to the pesto sauce and toss gently to coat. Serve immediately, scattered with the Parmesan cheese and accompanied by a rocket salad.

HELPFUL HINT

Use a vegetable peeler to pare the Parmesan cheese into decorative thin curls.

VEGETARIAN CASSOULET

INGREDIENTS   Serves 4

225 g/8 oz dried haricot beans,
   soaked overnight
2 medium onions
1 bay leaf
1.4 litres/2½ pints cold water
550 g/1¼ lb large potatoes,
   peeled and cut into 1 cm/
   ½ inch slices
salt and freshly ground black
   pepper
5 tsp olive oil
1 large garlic clove, peeled
   and crushed
2 leeks, trimmed and sliced

200 g can chopped tomatoes
1 tsp dark muscovado sugar
1 tbsp freshly chopped thyme
2 tbsp freshly chopped parsley
3 courgettes, trimmed and
   sliced

FOR THE TOPPING:
50 g/2 oz fresh white
   breadcrumbs
25 g/1oz Cheddar cheese,
   finely grated

1 Preheat the oven to 180°C/
350°F/Gas Mark 4, 10
minutes before required.
Drain the beans, rinse under
cold running water and put in a
saucepan. Peel 1 of the onions
and add to the beans with the
bay leaf. Pour in the water.

2 Bring to a rapid boil and
cook for 10 minutes, then
turn down the heat, cover and
simmer for 50 minutes, or until
the beans are almost tender.
Drain the beans, reserving the
liquor, but discarding the onion
and bay leaf.

3 Cook the potatoes in a
saucepan of lightly salted
boiling water for 6–7 minutes
until almost tender when tested
with the point of a knife. Drain
and reserve.

4 Peel and chop the remaining
onion. Heat the oil in a frying
pan and cook the onion with the
garlic and leeks for 10 minutes
until softened. Stir in the
tomatoes, sugar, thyme and
parsley. Stir in the beans, with
300 ml/½ pint of the reserved
liquor and season to taste.
Simmer, uncovered, for 5 minutes.

5 Layer the potato slices,
courgettes and ladlefuls of
the bean mixture in a large
flameproof casserole. To make
the topping, mix together the
breadcrumbs and cheese and
sprinkle over the top.

6 Bake in the preheated oven
for 40 minutes, or until the
vegetables are cooked through
and the topping is golden brown
and crisp. Serve immediately.

SWEET POTATO CAKES WITH MANGO & TOMATO SALSA

INGREDIENTS   Serves 4

700 g/1½ lb sweet potatoes, peeled and cut into large chunks

salt and freshly ground black pepper

25 g/1 oz butter

1 onion, peeled and chopped

1 garlic clove, peeled and crushed

pinch of freshly grated nutmeg

1 medium egg, beaten

50 g/2 oz quick-cook polenta

2 tbsp sunflower oil

FOR THE SALSA:

1 ripe mango, peeled, stoned and diced

6 cherry tomatoes, cut in wedges

4 spring onions, trimmed and thinly sliced

1 red chilli, deseeded and finely chopped

finely grated rind and juice of ½ lime

2 tbsp freshly chopped mint

1 tsp clear honey

salad leaves, to serve

1 Steam or cook the sweet potatoes in lightly salted boiling water for 15–20 minutes, until tender. Drain well, then mash until smooth.

2 Melt the butter in a saucepan. Add the onion and garlic and cook gently for 10 minutes until soft. Add to the mashed sweet potato and season with the nutmeg, salt and pepper. Stir together until mixed thoroughly. Leave to cool.

3 Shape the mixture into 4 oval potato cakes, about 2.5 cm/ 1 inch thick. Dip first in the beaten egg, allowing the excess to fall back into the bowl, then coat in the polenta. Refrigerate for at least 30 minutes.

4 Meanwhile, mix together all the ingredients for the salsa. Spoon into a serving bowl, cover with clingfilm and leave at room temperature to allow the flavours to develop.

5 Heat the oil in a frying pan and cook the potato cakes for 4–5 minutes on each side. Serve with the salsa and salad leaves.

FOOD FACT

Polenta is finely ground, golden cornmeal from Italy. It is often made into a soft, savoury mixture of the same name, but also makes an excellent coating for foods such as these potato cakes.

CHEESE & ONION OAT PIE

INGREDIENTS   Serves 4

1 tbsp sunflower oil, plus 1 tsp
25 g/1 oz butter
2 medium onions, peeled and
    sliced
1 garlic clove, peeled and
    crushed
150 g/5 oz porridge oats
125 g/4 oz mature Cheddar
    cheese, grated

2 medium eggs, lightly beaten
2 tbsp freshly chopped parsley
salt and freshly ground black
    pepper
275 g/10 oz baking potato,
    peeled

1 Preheat the oven to 180°C/ 350°F/Gas Mark 4. Heat the oil and half the butter in a saucepan until melted. Add the onions and garlic and gently cook for 10 minutes, or until soft. Remove from the heat and tip into a large bowl.

2 Spread the oats out on a baking sheet and toast in the hot oven for 12 minutes. Leave to cool, then add to the onions with the cheese, eggs and parsley. Season to taste with salt and pepper and mix well.

3 Line the base of a 20.5 cm/ 8 inch round sandwich tin with greaseproof paper and oil well. Thinly slice the potato and arrange the slices on the base, overlapping them slightly.

4 Spoon the cheese and oat mixture on top of the potato, spreading evenly with the back of a spoon. Cover with tinfoil and bake for 30 minutes.

5 Invert the pie onto a baking sheet so that the potatoes are on top. Carefully remove the tin and lining paper.

6 Preheat the grill to medium. Melt the remaining butter and carefully brush over the potato topping. Cook under the preheated grill for 5–6 minutes until the potatoes are lightly browned. Cut into wedges and serve.

TASTY TIP

To add flavour to this dish, cook the onions very slowly until soft and just beginning to colour and caramelise – either white or red onions can be used. For a crunchier texture, add 50 g/2 oz chopped hazelnuts instead of 50 g/2 oz of the oats, adding them to the baking sheet of oats for the last 5 minutes of cooking time, in step 2.

CHARGRILLED VEGETABLE & GOATS' CHEESE PIZZA

INGREDIENTS   Serves 4

125 g/4 oz baking potato
1 tbsp olive oil
225 g/8 oz strong white flour
½ tsp salt
1 tsp easy-blend dried yeast

FOR THE TOPPING:

1 medium aubergine, thinly
  sliced
2 small courgettes, trimmed
  and sliced lengthways
1 yellow pepper, quartered
  and deseeded

1 red onion, peeled and sliced
  into very thin wedges
5 tbsp olive oil
175 g/6 oz cooked new
  potatoes, halved
400 g can chopped tomatoes,
  drained
2 tsp freshly chopped oregano
125 g/4 oz mozzarella cheese,
  cut into small cubes
125 g/4 oz goats' cheese,
  crumbled

1 Preheat the oven to 220°C/425°F/Gas Mark 7, 15 minutes before baking. Put a baking sheet in the oven to heat up. Cook the potato in lightly salted boiling water until tender. Peel and mash with the olive oil until smooth.

2 Sift the flour and salt into a bowl. Stir in the yeast. Add the mashed potato and 150 ml/¼ pint warm water and mix to a soft dough. Knead for 5–6 minutes, until smooth. Put the dough in a bowl, cover with clingfilm and leave to rise in a warm place for 30 minutes.

3 To make the topping, arrange the aubergine, courgettes, pepper and onion, skin-side up, on a grill rack and brush with

4 tablespoons of the oil. Grill for 4–5 minutes. Turn the vegetables and brush with the remaining oil. Grill for 3–4 minutes. Cool, skin and slice the pepper. Put all of the vegetables in a bowl, add the halved new potatoes and toss gently together. Set aside.

4 Briefly re-knead the dough then roll out to a 30.5–35.5 cm/12–14 inch round, according to preferred thickness. Mix the tomatoes and oregano together and spread over the pizza base. Scatter over the mozzarella cheese. Put the pizza on the preheated baking sheet and bake for 8 minutes.

5 Arrange the vegetables and goats' cheese on top and bake for 8–10 minutes. Serve.

CHUNKY VEGETABLE & FENNEL GOULASH WITH DUMPLINGS

INGREDIENTS   Serves 4

2 fennel bulbs, weighing
   about 450 g/1 lb
2 tbsp sunflower oil
1 large onion, peeled and
   sliced
1½ tbsp paprika
1 tbsp plain flour
300 ml/½ pint vegetable stock
400 g can chopped tomatoes
450 g/1 lb potatoes, peeled
   and cut into 2.5 cm/1 inch
   chunks
125 g/4 oz small button
   mushrooms

salt and freshly ground black
   pepper

FOR THE DUMPLINGS:
1 tbsp sunflower oil
1 small onion, peeled and
   finely chopped
1 medium egg
3 tbsp milk
3 tbsp freshly chopped parsley
125 g/4 oz fresh white
   breadcrumbs

1 Cut the fennel bulbs in half widthways. Thickly slice the stalks and cut the bulbs into 8 wedges. Heat the oil in a large saucepan or flameproof casserole. Add the onion and fennel and cook gently for 10 minutes until soft. Stir in the paprika and flour.

2 Remove from the heat and gradually stir in the stock. Add the chopped tomatoes, potatoes and mushrooms. Season to taste with salt and pepper. Bring to the boil, reduce the heat and simmer for 20 minutes.

3 Meanwhile, make the dumplings. Heat the oil in a frying pan and gently cook the onion for 10 minutes, until soft. Leave to cool for a few minutes.

4 In a bowl, beat the egg and milk together, then add the onion, parsley, breadcrumbs, and season to taste. With damp hands form the breadcrumb mixture into 12 round dumplings each about the size of a walnut.

5 Arrange the dumplings on top of the goulash. Cover and cook for a further 15 minutes, until the dumplings are cooked and the vegetables are tender. Serve immediately.

TASTY TIP

Soured cream or
crème fraîche would be
delicious if spooned on
top of the goulash.

CREAMY VEGETABLE KORMA

INGREDIENTS   Serves 4–6

2 tbsp ghee or vegetable oil
1 large onion, peeled and
  chopped
2 garlic cloves, peeled and
  crushed
2.5 cm/1 inch piece of root
  ginger, peeled and grated
4 cardamom pods
2 tsp ground coriander
1 tsp ground cumin
1 tsp ground turmeric
finely grated rind and juice of
  ½ lemon

50 g/2 oz ground almonds
400 ml/14 fl oz vegetable stock
450 g/1 lb potatoes, peeled
  and diced
450 g/1 lb mixed vegetables,
  such as cauliflower, carrots
  and turnip, cut into chunks
150 ml/¼ pint double cream
3 tbsp freshly chopped
  coriander
salt and freshly ground black
  pepper
naan bread, to serve

1 Heat the ghee or oil in a large saucepan. Add the onion and cook for 5 minutes. Stir in the garlic and ginger and cook for a further 5 minutes, or until soft and just beginning to colour.

2 Stir in the cardamom, ground coriander, cumin and turmeric. Continue cooking over a low heat for 1 minute, stirring.

3 Stir in the lemon rind and juice and almonds. Blend in the vegetable stock. Slowly bring to the boil, stirring occasionally.

4 Add the potatoes and vegetables. Bring back to the boil, then reduce the heat, cover and simmer for 35–40 minutes, or until the vegetables are just tender. Check after 25 minutes and add a little more stock if needed.

5 Slowly stir in the cream and chopped coriander. Season to taste with salt and pepper. Cook very gently until heated through, but do not boil. Serve immediately with naan bread.

FOOD FACT

Ghee is butter, clarified by gently heating until all the water has been evaporated and the milk solids separated from the pure fat, which can be used to cook at high temperatures without burning. You can buy butter-based ghee as well as a vegetarian version in specialist shops and Indian groceries.

CABBAGE TIMBALE

INGREDIENTS   Serves 4–6

1 small savoy cabbage,
  weighing about 350 g/12 oz
salt and freshly ground black
  pepper
2 tbsp olive oil
1 leek, trimmed and chopped
1 garlic clove, peeled and
  crushed
75 g/3 oz long-grain rice
200 g can chopped tomatoes

300 ml/½ pint vegetable stock
400 g can flageolet beans,
  drained and rinsed
75 g/3 oz Cheddar cheese,
  grated
1 tbsp freshly chopped oregano

TO GARNISH:
Greek yogurt with paprika
tomato wedges

1 Preheat the oven to 180°C/ 350°F/Gas Mark 4, 10 minutes before required. Remove 6 of the outer leaves of the cabbage. Cut off the thickest part of the stalk and blanch the leaves in lightly salted boiling water for 2 minutes. Lift out with a slotted spoon and briefly rinse under cold water and reserve.

2 Remove the stalks from the rest of the cabbage leaves. Shred the leaves and blanch in the boiling water for 1 minute. Drain, rinse under cold water and pat dry on absorbent kitchen paper.

3 Heat the oil in a frying pan and cook the leek and garlic for 5 minutes. Stir in the rice, chopped tomatoes with their juice and stock. Bring to the boil, cover and simmer for 15 minutes.

4 Remove the lid and simmer for a further 4–5 minutes, stirring frequently, until the

liquid is absorbed and the rice is tender. Stir in the flageolet beans, cheese and oregano. Season to taste with salt and pepper.

5 Line an oiled 1.1 litre/2 pint pudding basin with some of the large cabbage leaves, overlapping them slightly. Fill the basin with alternate layers of rice mixture and shredded leaves, pressing down well.

6 Cover the top with the remaining leaves. Cover with oiled tinfoil and bake in the preheated for 30 minutes. Leave to stand for 10 minutes. Turn out, cut into wedges and serve with yogurt sprinkled with paprika and tomato wedges.

HANDY HINT

Avoid red or white cabbage
for this recipe as their leaves
are not flexible enough.

INDONESIAN SALAD WITH PEANUT DRESSING

INGREDIENTS   Serves 4

225 g/8 oz new potatoes, scrubbed

1 large carrot, peeled and cut into matchsticks

125 g/4 oz French beans, trimmed

225 g/8 oz tiny cauliflower florets

125 g/4 oz cucumber, cut into matchsticks

75 g/3 oz fresh bean sprouts

3 medium eggs, hard-boiled and quartered

FOR THE PEANUT DRESSING:

2 tbsp sesame oil

1 garlic clove, peeled and crushed

1 red chilli, deseeded and finely chopped

150 g/5 oz crunchy peanut butter

6 tbsp hot vegetable stock

2 tsp soft light brown sugar

2 tsp dark soy sauce

1 tbsp lime juice

1 Cook the potatoes in a saucepan of boiling salted water for 15–20 minutes until tender. Remove with a slotted spoon and thickly slice into a large bowl. Keep the saucepan of water boiling.

2 Add the carrot, French beans and cauliflower to the water, return to the boil and cook for 2 minutes, or until just tender. Drain and refresh under cold running water, then drain well. Add to the potatoes with the cucumber and bean sprouts.

3 To make the dressing, gently heat the sesame oil in a small saucepan. Add the garlic and chilli and cook for a few seconds, then remove from the heat. Stir in the peanut butter.

4 Stir in the stock, a little at a time. Add the remaining ingredients and mix together to make a thick, creamy dressing.

5 Divide the vegetables between 4 plates and arrange the eggs on top. Drizzle the dressing over the salad and serve immediately.

HELPFUL HINT

For perfect hard-boiled eggs, put in a saucepan of cold water and simmer gently for 9 minutes, turning once or twice during the first 2 minutes so that the yolks stay central, then plunge straight away into cold water to stop black rings forming around the yolks.

LAYERED CHEESE & HERB POTATO CAKE

INGREDIENTS   Serves 4

900 g/2 lb waxy potatoes
3 tbsp freshly snipped chives
2 tbsp freshly chopped parsley
225 g/8 oz mature Cheddar
  cheese
2 large egg yolks
1 tsp paprika
125 g/4 oz fresh white
  breadcrumbs

50 g/2 oz almonds, toasted
  and roughly chopped
50 g/2 oz butter, melted
salt and freshly ground black
  pepper
mixed salad or steamed
  vegetables, to serve

1 Preheat the oven to 180°C/ 350°F/Gas Mark 4. Lightly oil and line the base of a 20.5 cm/ 8 inch round cake tin with lightly oiled greaseproof or baking parchment paper. Peel and thinly slice the potatoes and reserve. Stir the chives, parsley, cheese and egg yolks together in a small bowl and reserve. Mix the paprika into the breadcrumbs.

2 Sprinkle the almonds over the base of the lined tin. Cover with half the potatoes, arranging them in layers, then sprinkle with the paprika bread-crumb mixture and season to taste with salt and pepper.

3 Spoon the cheese and herb mixture over the bread-crumbs with a little more seasoning, then arrange the remaining potatoes on top. Drizzle over the melted butter and press the surface down firmly.

4 Bake in the preheated oven for 1¼ hours, or until golden and cooked through. Let the tin stand for 10 minutes before carefully turning out and serving in thick wedges. Serve immediately with salad or freshly cooked vegetables.

HANDY HINT

Check that the potatoes are tender all the way through by pushing a thin skewer through the centre. If the potatoes are still a little hard and the top is already brown enough, loosely cover with a piece of tinfoil and continue cooking until done.

BABY ROAST POTATO SALAD

INGREDIENTS

Serves 4

350 g/12 oz small shallots
sea salt and freshly ground
    black pepper
900 g/2 lb small even-sized
    new potatoes
2 tbsp olive oil
2 medium courgettes

2 sprigs of fresh rosemary
175 g/6 oz cherry tomatoes
150 ml/¼ pint soured cream
2 tbsp freshly snipped chives
¼ tsp paprika

1 Preheat the oven to 200°C/ 400°F/Gas Mark 6. Trim the shallots, but leave the skins on. Put in a saucepan of lightly salted boiling water with the potatoes and cook for 5 minutes; drain. Separate the shallots and plunge them into cold water for 1 minute.

2 Put the oil in a baking sheet lined with tinfoil or roasting tin and heat for a few minutes. Peel the skins off the shallots – they should now come away easily. Add to the baking sheet or roasting tin with the potatoes and toss in the oil to coat. Sprinkle with a little sea salt. Roast the potatoes and shallots in the preheated oven for 10 minutes.

3 Meanwhile, trim the courgettes, halve lengthways and cut into 5 cm/2 inch chunks. Add to the baking sheet or roasting tin, toss to mix and cook for 5 minutes.

4 Pierce the tomato skins with a sharp knife. Add to the sheet or tin with the rosemary and cook for a further 5 minutes, or until all the vegetables are tender. Remove the rosemary and discard. Grind a little black pepper over the vegetables.

5 Spoon into a wide serving bowl. Mix together the soured cream and chives and drizzle over the vegetables just before serving.

TASTY TIP

For a more substantial salad or to serve 6 rather than 4 people, add 225 g/8 oz baby aubergines, cut in half length-ways and cook with the potatoes and shallots, along with an extra 1 tablespoon olive oil. If you prefer, crème fraîche or Greek-style yogurt may be used instead of the soured cream.

RICE NUGGETS IN HERBY TOMATO SAUCE

INGREDIENTS Serves 4

600 ml/1 pint vegetable stock
1 bay leaf
175 g/6 oz Arborio rice
50 g/2 oz Cheddar cheese,
  grated
1 medium egg yolk
1 tbsp plain flour
2 tbsp freshly chopped parsley
salt and freshly ground black
  pepper
grated Parmesan cheese, to
  serve

**FOR THE HERBY TOMATO
  SAUCE:**
1 tbsp olive oil
1 onion, peeled and thinly
  sliced
1 garlic clove, peeled and
  crushed
1 small yellow pepper,
  deseeded and diced
400 g can chopped tomatoes
1 tbsp freshly chopped basil

1 Pour the stock into a large saucepan. Add the bay leaf. Bring to the boil, add the rice, stir, then cover and simmer for 15 minutes.

2 Uncover, reduce the heat to low and cook for a further 5 minutes until the rice is tender and all the stock is absorbed, stirring frequently towards the end of cooking time. Cool.

3 Stir the cheese, egg yolk, flour and parsley into the rice. Season to taste, then shape into 20 walnut-sized balls. Cover and refrigerate.

4 To make the sauce, heat the oil in a large frying pan and cook the onion for 5 minutes. Add the garlic and yellow pepper and cook for a further 5 minutes, until soft.

5 Stir in the chopped tomatoes and simmer gently for 3 minutes. Stir in the chopped basil and season to taste.

6 Add the rice nuggets to the sauce and simmer for a further 10 minutes, or until the rice nuggets are cooked through and the sauce has reduced a little. Spoon onto serving plates and serve hot, sprinkled with grated Parmesan cheese.

HELPFUL HINT

It is important that the stock is absorbed completely by the rice if these nuggets are to hold their shape. Stir all the time for the last minute of cooking to prevent the rice from sticking or burning.

MIXED GRAIN PILAF

INGREDIENTS   Serves 4

2 tbsp olive oil

1 garlic clove, peeled and
  crushed

½ tsp ground turmeric

125 g/4 oz mixed long-grain
  and wild rice

50 g/2 oz red lentils

300 ml/½ pint vegetable stock

200 g can chopped tomatoes

5 cm/2 inch piece cinnamon
  stick

salt and freshly ground black
  pepper

400 g can mixed beans,
  drained and rinsed

15 g/½ oz butter

1 bunch spring onions,
  trimmed and finely sliced

3 medium eggs

4 tbsp freshly chopped herbs,
  such as parsley and chervil

sprigs of fresh dill, to garnish

1 Heat 1 tablespoon of the oil in a saucepan. Add the garlic and turmeric and cook for a few seconds. Stir in the rice and lentils.

2 Add the stock, tomatoes and cinnamon. Season to taste with salt and pepper. Stir once and bring to the boil. Lower the heat, cover and simmer for 20 minutes, until most of the stock is absorbed and the rice and lentils are tender.

3 Stir in the beans, replace the lid and leave to stand for 2–3 minutes to allow the beans to heat through.

4 While the rice is cooking, heat the remaining oil and butter in a frying pan. Add the spring onions and cook for 4–5 minutes, until soft. Lightly beat the eggs with 2 tablespoons of the herbs, then season with salt and pepper.

5 Pour the egg mixture over the spring onions. Stir gently with a spatula over a low heat, drawing the mixture from the sides to the centre as the omelette sets. When almost set, stop stirring and cook for about 30 seconds until golden underneath.

6 Remove the omelette from the pan, roll up and slice into thin strips. Fluff the rice up with a fork and remove the cinnamon stick. Spoon onto serving plates, top with strips of omelette and the remaining chopped herbs. Garnish with sprigs of dill and serve.

HELPFUL HINT

Long-grain rice and wild rice have different cooking times, but in ready-mixed packets, the rice has been treated to even out the cooking times, making preparation simpler.

CALYPSO RICE WITH CURRIED BANANAS

INGREDIENTS   Serves 4

2 tbsp sunflower oil
1 medium onion, peeled and
   finely chopped
1 garlic clove, peeled and
   crushed
1 red chilli, deseeded and
   finely chopped
1 red pepper, deseeded and
   chopped
225 g/8 oz basmati rice
juice of 1 lime
350 ml/12 fl oz vegetable stock

200 g can black-eye beans,
   drained and rinsed
2 tbsp freshly chopped parsley
salt and freshly ground black
   pepper
sprigs of coriander, to garnish

FOR THE CURRIED BANANAS:
4 green bananas
2 tbsp sunflower oil
2 tsp mild curry paste
200 ml/7 fl oz coconut milk

1 Heat the oil in a large frying pan and gently cook the onion, for 10 minutes until soft. Add the garlic, chilli and red pepper and cook for 2–3 minutes.

2 Rinse the rice under cold running water, then add to the pan and stir. Pour in the lime juice and stock, bring to the boil, cover and simmer for 12–15 minutes, or until the rice is tender and the stock is absorbed.

3 Stir in the black-eye beans and chopped parsley and season to taste with salt and pepper. Leave to stand, covered, for 5 minutes before serving, to allow the beans to warm through.

4 While the rice is cooking, make the curried green

bananas. Remove the skins from the bananas – they may need to be cut off with a sharp knife. Slice the flesh thickly. Heat the oil in a frying pan and cook the bananas, in 2 batches, for 2–3 minutes, or until lightly browned.

5 Pour the coconut milk into the pan and stir in the curry paste.

6 Add the banana slices to the coconut milk and simmer, uncovered, over a low heat for 8–10 minutes, or until the bananas are very soft and the coconut milk slightly reduced.

7 Spoon the rice onto warmed serving plates, garnish with coriander and serve immediately with the curried bananas.

RED LENTIL KEDGEREE WITH AVOCADO & TOMATOES

INGREDIENTS   Serves 4

150 g/5 oz basmati rice
150 g/5 oz red lentils
15 g/½ oz butter
1 tbsp sunflower oil
1 medium onion, peeled and
  chopped
1 tsp ground cumin
4 cardamom pods, bruised
1 bay leaf
450 ml/¾ pint vegetable stock
1 ripe avocado, peeled, stoned
  and diced

1 tbsp lemon juice
4 plum tomatoes, peeled and
  diced
2 tbsp freshly chopped
  coriander
salt and freshly ground black
  pepper
lemon or lime slices, to
  garnish

1 Put the rice and lentils in a sieve and rinse under cold running water. Tip into a bowl, then pour over enough cold water to cover and leave to soak for 10 minutes.

2 Heat the butter and oil in a saucepan. Add the sliced onion and cook gently, stirring occasionally, for 10 minutes until softened. Stir in the cumin, cardamon pods and bay leaf and cook for a further minute, stirring all the time.

3 Drain the rice and lentils, rinse again and add to the onions in the saucepan. Stir in the vegetable stock and bring to the boil. Reduce the heat, cover the saucepan and simmer for 14–15 minutes, or until the rice and lentils are tender.

4 Place the diced avocado in a bowl and toss with the lemon juice. Stir in the tomatoes and chopped coriander. Season to taste with salt and pepper.

5 Fluff up the rice with a fork, spoon into a warmed serving dish and spoon the avocado mixture on top. Garnish with lemon or lime slices and serve.

TASTY TIP

Although basmati rice and red lentils do not usually need to be pre-soaked, it improves the results of this recipe: the rice will cook to very light, fluffy separate grains and the lentils will just begin to break down giving the dish a creamier texture.

ADUKI BEAN & RICE BURGERS

INGREDIENTS   Serves 4

2½ tbsp sunflower oil

1 medium onion, peeled and
very finely chopped

1 garlic clove, peeled and
crushed

1 tsp curry paste

225 g/8 oz basmati rice

400 g can aduki beans,
drained and rinsed

225 ml/8 fl oz vegetable stock

125 g/4 oz firm tofu, crumbled

1 tsp garam masala

2 tbsp freshly chopped
coriander

salt and freshly ground black
pepper

FOR THE CARROT RAITA:

2 large carrots, peeled and
grated

½ cucumber, cut into tiny dice

150 ml/¼ pint Greek yogurt

TO SERVE:

wholemeal baps

tomato slices

lettuce leaves

1 Heat 1 tablespoon of the oil in a saucepan and gently cook the onion for 10 minutes until soft. Add the garlic and curry paste and cook for a few more seconds. Stir in the rice and beans.

2 Pour in the stock, bring to the boil and simmer for 12 minutes, or until all the stock has been absorbed – do not lift the lid for the first 10 minutes of cooking. Reserve.

3 Lightly mash the tofu. Add to the rice mixture with the garam masala, coriander, salt and pepper. Mix.

4 Divide the mixture into 8 and shape into burgers. Chill in the refrigerator for 30 minutes.

5 Meanwhile, make the raita. Mix together the carrots, cucumber and Greek yogurt. Spoon into a small bowl and chill in the refrigerator until ready to serve.

6 Heat the remaining oil in a large frying pan. Fry the burgers, in batches if necessary, for 4–5 minutes on each side, or until lightly browned. Serve in the baps with tomato slices and lettuce. Accompany with the raita.

FOOD FACT

Firm tofu is sold in blocks. It is made in a similar way to soft cheese and is the pressed curds of soya milk.

WILD RICE DOLMADES

INGREDIENTS

Serves 4–6

6 tbsp olive oil
25 g/1 oz pine nuts
175 g/6 oz mushrooms, wiped and finely chopped
4 spring onions, trimmed and finely chopped
1 garlic clove, peeled and crushed
50 g/2 oz cooked wild rice
2 tsp freshly chopped dill
2 tsp freshly chopped mint

salt and freshly ground black pepper
16–24 prepared medium vine leaves
about 300 ml/½ pint vegetable stock

TO GARNISH:
lemon wedges
sprigs of fresh dill

1 Heat 1 tbsp of the oil in a frying pan and gently cook the pine nuts for 2–3 minutes, stirring frequently, until golden. Remove from the pan and reserve.

2 Add 1½ tablespoons of oil to the pan and gently cook the mushrooms, spring onions and garlic for 7–8 minutes until very soft. Stir in the rice, herbs, salt and pepper.

3 Put a heaped teaspoon of stuffing in the centre of each leaf (if the leaves are small, put 2 together, overlapping slightly). Fold over the stalk end, then the sides and roll up to make a neat parcel. Continue until all the stuffing is used.

4 Arrange the stuffed vine leaves close together seam-side down in a large saucepan, drizzling each with a little of the remaining oil – there will be several layers. Pour over just enough stock to cover.

5 Put an inverted plate over the dolmades to stop them unrolling during cooking. Bring to the boil, then simmer very gently for 3 minutes. Cool in the saucepan.

6 Transfer the dolmades to a serving dish. Cover and chill in the refrigerator before serving. Sprinkle with the pine nuts and garnish with lemon and dill. Serve.

HELPFUL HINT

Fresh vine leaves are available in early summer and should be blanched for 2–3 minutes in boiling water. Vine leaves preserved in brine can be found all year round in super-markets – soak in warm water for 20 minutes before using.

Broad Bean & Artichoke Risotto

INGREDIENTS   Serves 4

275 g/10 oz frozen broad
  beans

400 g can artichoke hearts,
  drained

1 tbsp sunflower oil

150 ml/¼ pint dry white wine

900 ml/1½ pints vegetable
  stock

25 g/1 oz butter

1 onion, peeled and finely
  chopped

200 g/7 oz Arborio rice

finely grated rind and juice of
  1 lemon

50 g/2 oz Parmesan cheese,
  grated

salt and freshly ground black
  pepper

freshly grated Parmesan
  cheese, to serve

1 Cook the beans in a saucepan of lightly salted boiling water for 4–5 minutes, or until just tender. Drain and plunge into cold water. Peel off the tough outer skins, if liked. Pat the artichokes dry on absorbent kitchen paper and cut each in half lengthways through the stem end. Cut each half into 3 wedges.

2 Heat the oil in a large saucepan and cook the artichokes for 4–5 minutes, turning occasionally, until they are lightly browned. Remove and reserve. Bring the wine and stock to the boil in a separate frying pan. Keep them barely simmering while making the risotto.

3 Melt the butter in a large frying pan, add the onion and cook for 5 minutes until beginning to soften. Add the rice and cook for

1 minute, stirring. Pour in a ladleful of the hot wine and stock, simmer gently, stirring frequently, until the stock is absorbed. Continue to add the stock in this way for 20–25 minutes, until the rice is just tender; the risotto should look creamy and soft.

4 Add the broad beans, artichokes, and lemon rind and juice. Gently mix in, cover and leave to warm through for 1–2 minutes. Stir in the Parmesan cheese and season to taste with salt and pepper. Serve sprinkled with extra Parmesan cheese.

HELPFUL HINT

If using fresh broad beans, buy about 700 g/1½ lb in their pods. Young fresh beans do not need to be skinned.

MEDITERRANEAN RICE SALAD

INGREDIENTS   Serves 4

250 g/9 oz Camargue red rice

2 sun-dried tomatoes, finely chopped

2 garlic cloves, peeled and finely chopped

4 tbsp oil from a jar of sun-dried tomatoes

2 tsp balsamic vinegar

2 tsp red wine vinegar

salt and freshly ground black pepper

1 red onion, peeled and thinly sliced

1 yellow pepper, quartered and deseeded

1 red pepper, quartered and deseeded

½ cucumber, peeled and diced

6 ripe plum tomatoes, cut into wedges

1 fennel bulb, halved and thinly sliced

fresh basil leaves, to garnish

1 Cook the rice in a saucepan of lightly salted boiling water for 35–40 minutes, or until tender. Drain well and reserve.

2 Whisk the sun-dried tomatoes, garlic, oil and vinegars together in a small bowl or jug. Season to taste with salt and pepper. Put the red onion in a large bowl, pour over the dressing and leave to allow the flavours to develop.

3 Put the peppers, skin-side up on a grill rack and cook under a preheated hot grill for 5–6 minutes, or until blackened and charred. Remove and place in a plastic bag. When cool enough to handle, peel off the skins and slice the peppers.

4 Add the peppers, cucumber, tomatoes, fennel and rice to the onions. Mix gently together to coat in the dressing. Cover and chill in the refrigerator for 30 minutes to allow the flavours to mingle.

5 Remove the salad from the refrigerator and leave to stand at room temperature for 20 minutes. Garnish with fresh basil leaves and serve.

FOOD FACT

Camargue red rice from the south of France is a reddish-brown colour and gives this salad a stunning appearance. It has a texture and cooking time similar to that of brown rice, which may be substituted in this recipe if Camargue red rice is unavailable.

CHEF'S RICE SALAD

INGREDIENTS   Serves 4

225 g/8 oz wild rice

½ cucumber

175 g/6 oz cherry tomatoes

6 spring onions, trimmed

5 tbsp extra-virgin olive oil

2 tbsp balsamic vinegar

1 tsp Dijon mustard

1 tsp caster sugar

salt and freshly ground black
   pepper

125 g/4 oz rocket

125 g/4 oz back bacon

125 g/4 oz cooked chicken
   meat, finely diced

125 g/4 oz Emmenthal cheese,
   grated

125 g/4 oz large cooked
   prawns, peeled

1 avocado, stoned, peeled and
   sliced, to garnish

warm crusty bread, to serve

1 Put the rice in in a saucepan of water and bring to the boil, stirring once or twice. Reduce the heat, cover and simmer gently for 30–50 minutes, depending on the texture you prefer. Drain well and reserve.

2 Thinly peel the cucumber, cut in half, then using a teaspoon, remove the seeds. Cut the cucumber into thin slices. Cut the tomatoes in quarters. Cut the spring onions into diagonal slices.

3 Whisk the olive oil with the vinegar, then whisk in the mustard and sugar. Season to taste with salt and pepper.

4 In a large bowl, gently toss together the cooled rice with the tomatoes, cucumber, spring onions and the rocket. Pour over the dressing and toss lightly together.

5 Heat a griddle pan and when hot cook the bacon on both sides for 4–6 minutes, or until crisp. Remove and chop. Arrange the prepared rocket salad on a platter, then arrange the bacon, chicken, cheese and prawns on top. Toss, if wished. Garnish with avocado slices and serve with plenty of warm, crusty bread.

TASTY TIP

You can use any combination of your favourite cold meats in this salad; smoked duck or chicken work particularly well. Emmenthal cheese, famous for its large, round holes, has a mellow and sweet flavour that is good in this salad, or you can use an alternative hard cheese, such as Jarlsberg, Gouda or Gruyère.

RICE WITH SMOKED SALMON & GINGER

INGREDIENTS   Serves 4

225 g/8 oz basmati rice
600 ml/1 pint fish stock
1 bunch spring onions,
   trimmed and diagonally
   sliced
3 tbsp freshly chopped
   coriander
1 tsp grated fresh root ginger

200 g/7 oz sliced smoked
   salmon
2 tbsp soy sauce
1 tsp sesame oil
2 tsp lemon juice
4–6 slices pickled ginger
2 tsp sesame seeds
rocket leaves, to serve

1 Place the rice in a sieve and rinse under cold water until the water runs clear. Drain, then place in a large saucepan with the stock and bring gently to the boil. Reduce to a simmer and cover with a tight-fitting lid. Cook for 10 minutes, then remove from the heat and leave, covered, for a further 10 minutes.

2 Stir the spring onions, coriander and fresh ginger into the cooked rice and mix well.

3 Spoon the rice into 4 tartlet tins, each measuring 10 cm/ 4 inches, and press down firmly with the back of a spoon to form cakes. Invert a tin onto an individual serving plate, then tap the base firmly and remove the tin. Repeat with the rest of the filled tins.

4 Top the rice with the salmon, folding if necessary, so the sides of the rice can still be seen in places. Mix together the soy sauce, sesame oil and lemon juice to make a dressing, then drizzle over the salmon. Top with the pickled ginger and a sprinkling of sesame seeds. Scatter the rocket leaves around the edge of the plates and serve immediately.

FOOD FACT

Good smoked salmon should look moist and firm and have a peachy pink colour. If you buy it from a delicatessan counter, ask for it to be freshly sliced as any that has already been sliced may be dried out. Vacuum-packed salmon will keep for about 2 weeks in the refrigerator (check the use-by date), but once opened should be used within 3 days.

SWEET & SOUR RICE WITH CHICKEN

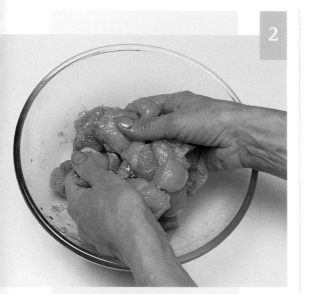

INGREDIENTS
Serves 4

4 spring onions
2 tsp sesame oil
1 tsp Chinese five-spice
powder
450 g/1 lb chicken breast, cut
into cubes
1 tbsp oil
1 garlic clove, peeled and
crushed
1 medium onion, peeled and
sliced into thin wedges

225 g/8 oz long-grain white
rice
600 ml/1 pint water
4 tbsp tomato ketchup
1 tbsp tomato purée
2 tbsp honey
1 tbsp vinegar
1 tbsp dark soy sauce
1 carrot, peeled and cut into
matchsticks

1 Trim the spring onions, then cut lengthways into fine strips. Drop into a large bowl of iced water and reserve.

2 Mix together the sesame oil and Chinese five-spice powder and use to rub into the cubed chicken. Heat the wok, then add the oil and when hot, cook the garlic and onion for 2–3 minutes, or until transparent and softened.

3 Add the chicken and stir-fry over a medium-high heat until the chicken is golden and cooked through. Using a slotted spoon, remove from the wok and keep warm.

4 Stir the rice into the wok and add the water, tomato ketchup, tomato purée, honey, vinegar and soy sauce. Stir well to

mix. Bring to the boil, then simmer until almost all of the liquid is absorbed. Stir in the carrot and reserved chicken and continue to cook for 3–4 minutes.

5 Drain the spring onions, which will have become curly. Garnish with the spring onion curls and serve immediately with the rice and chicken.

FOOD FACT

Five-spice powder is a popular Chinese seasoning that can be bought ready-blended in jars in most super-markets. It is a mixture of finely ground star anise, fennel, cinnamon, cloves and Sichuan pepper and adds a unique sweet and spicy aniseed flavour to food.

SALMON & FILO PARCELS

INGREDIENTS
Serves 4

1 tbsp sunflower oil
1 bunch of spring onions,
  trimmed and finely chopped
1 tsp paprika
175 g/6 oz long-grain white
  rice
300 ml/½ pint fish stock
salt and freshly ground black
  pepper

450 g/1 lb salmon fillet, cubed
1 tbsp freshly chopped parsley
grated rind and juice of 1
  lemon
150 g/5 oz rocket
150 g/5 oz spinach
12 sheets filo pastry
50 g/2 oz butter, melted

1 Preheat the oven to 200°C/ 400°F/Gas Mark 6. Heat the oil in a small frying pan and gently cook the spring onions for 2 minutes. Stir in the paprika and continue to cook for 1 minute, then remove from the heat and reserve.

2 Put the rice in a sieve and rinse under cold running water until the water runs clear; drain. Put the rice and stock in a saucepan, bring to the boil, then cover and simmer for 10 minutes, or until the liquid is absorbed and the rice is tender. Add the spring onion mixture and fork through. Season to taste with salt and pepper, then leave to cool.

3 In a non-metallic bowl, mix together the salmon, parsley, lemon rind and juice and salt and pepper. Reserve.

4 Blanch the rocket and spinach for 30 seconds in a large saucepan of boiling water, or until just wilted. Drain well in a colander and refresh in plenty of cold water, then squeeze out as much moisture as possible.

4 Brush 3 sheets of filo pastry with melted butter and lay them on top of one another. Take a quarter of the rice mixture and arrange it in an oblong in the centre of the pastry. On top of this place a quarter of the salmon followed by a quarter of the rocket and spinach.

5 Draw up the pastry around the filling and twist at the top to create a parcel. Repeat with the remaining pastry and filling until you have 4 parcels. Brush with the remaining butter.

6 Place the parcels on a lightly oiled baking tray and cook in the preheated oven for 20 minutes, or until golden brown and cooked. Serve immediately.

WILD MUSHROOM RISOTTO

INGREDIENTS   Serves 4

15 g/½ oz dried porcini
1.1 litres/2 pints vegetable
   stock
75 g/3 oz butter
1 tbsp olive oil
1 onion, peeled and chopped
2–4 garlic cloves, peeled and
   chopped
1–2 red chillies, deseeded and
   chopped
225 g/8 oz wild mushrooms,
   wiped and halved, if large

125 g/4 oz button mushrooms,
   wiped and sliced
350 g/12 oz Arborio rice
175 g/6 oz large cooked
   prawns, peeled
150 ml/¼ pint white wine
salt and freshly ground black
   pepper
1 tbsp lemon zest
1 tbsp freshly snipped chives
2 tbsp freshly chopped parsley

1 Soak the porcini in 300 ml/ ½ pint of very hot, but not boiling water for 30 minutes. Drain, reserving the mushrooms and soaking liquid. Pour the stock into a saucepan, and bring to the boil, then reduce the heat to keep it simmering.

2 Melt the butter and oil in a large deep frying pan, add the onion, garlic and chillies and cook gently for 5 minutes. Add the wild and button mushrooms with the drained porcini, and continue to cook for 4–5 minutes, stirring frequently.

3 Stir in the rice and cook for 1 minute. Strain the reserved soaking liquid and stir into the rice with a little of the hot stock. Cook gently, stirring frequently, until the liquid is absorbed. Continue to add most of the stock, a ladleful at a time,

cooking after each addition, until the rice is tender and the risotto looks creamy.

4 Add the prawns and wine along with the last additions of stock. When the prawns are hot and all the liquid is absorbed, season to taste with salt and pepper. Remove from the heat and stir in the lemon zest, chives and parsley, reserving some for the garnish. Garnish and serve.

FOOD FACT

Ceps are wild mushrooms, also known by their Italian name *porcini*. They have a meaty texture and an almost woody taste. Dried ceps are expensive, but you only need the tiniest amount to add an incredibly intense mushroom flavour to this risotto.

SPECIAL FRIED RICE

INGREDIENTS   Serves 4

1 large egg

1 tsp sesame oil

350 g/8 oz long-grain white rice

1 tbsp groundnut oil

450 g/1 lb boneless, skinless chicken breast, diced

8 spring onions, trimmed and sliced

2 large carrots, trimmed and cut into matchsticks

125 g/4 oz sugar snap peas

125 g/4 oz raw tiger prawns, peeled

2 tsp Chinese five-spice powder

1 tbsp soy sauce

1 tbsp Thai fish sauce

1 tbsp rice wine vinegar

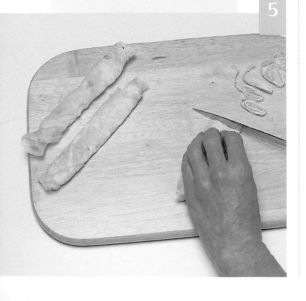

1 Beat the egg in a bowl with ½ teaspoon of the sesame oil and 2 teaspoons of water. Heat a frying pan over a medium-high heat and swirl in 2 tablespoons of the egg mixture to form a paper-thin omelette. Remove and reserve. Repeat this process until all the egg has been used.

2 Cook the rice in lightly salted boiling water for 12 minutes, or until tender. Drain and reserve.

3 Heat a wok, then add the remaining sesame oil with the groundnut oil and stir-fry the chicken for 5 minutes until cooked through. Using a slotted spoon, remove from the wok and keep warm.

4 Add the spring onions, carrot and sugar snap peas to the wok and stir-fry for 2–3 minutes.

Add the prawns and stir-fry for 2–3 minutes, or until pink. Return the chicken to the wok with the Chinese five-spice powder and stir-fry for 1 minute. Stir in the drained rice.

5 Mix together the soy sauce, fish sauce and vinegar. Pour into the wok and continue to stir-fry for 2–3 minutes. Roll the papery omelettes into tight rolls and slice to form thin strips. Stir into the rice and serve immediately.

FOOD FACT

A classic Chinese ingredient, sesame oil is richly coloured and strongly flavoured. It has a low smoking temperature, so should not be heated to an extremely high temperature, otherwise the delicious sesame flavour will be lost.

LEG OF LAMB WITH MINTED RICE

INGREDIENTS   Serves 4

1 tbsp olive oil
1 medium onion, peeled and
  finely chopped
1 garlic clove, peeled and
  crushed
1 celery stalk, trimmed and
  chopped
1 large mild red chilli,
  deseeded and chopped

75 g/3 oz long-grain rice
150 ml/¼ pint lamb or chicken
  stock
2 tbsp freshly chopped mint
salt and freshly ground black
  pepper
1.4 kg/3 lb boned leg of lamb
freshly cooked vegetables, to
  serve

1 Preheat the oven to 190°C/
375°F/Gas Mark 5, 10
minutes before roasting. Heat
the oil in a frying pan and gently
cook the onion for 5 minutes.
Stir in the garlic, celery and
chilli and continue to cook for
3–4 minutes.

2 Place the rice and the stock
in a large saucepan and cook,
covered, for 10–12 minutes or
until the rice is tender and all
the liquid is absorbed. Stir in the
onion and celery mixture, then
leave to cool. Once the rice
mixture is cold, stir in the
chopped mint and season to
taste with salt and pepper.

3 Place the boned lamb skin-
side down and spoon the rice
mixture along the centre of the
meat. Roll up the meat to enclose
the stuffing and tie securely with
string. Place in a roasting tin and
roast in the preheated oven for

1 hour 20 minutes, or until
cooked to personal preference.
Remove from the oven and
leave to rest in a warm place
for 20 minutes, before carving.
Serve with a selection of
cooked vegetables.

HELPFUL HINT

Weigh the lamb after stuffing
and allow it to come to room
temperature before roasting.
For medium-cooked lamb,
allow 25 minutes per 450 g/
1 lb plus 25 minutes; for well-
done, allow 30 minutes per
450 g/1 lb plus 30 minutes.
Use a meat thermometer to
check whether the joint is
cooked, or push a fine skewer
into the thickest part: for rare
meat the juices will be
slightly red, for medium they
will be pink and when well-
done, the juices will run clear.

LEMON CHICKEN RICE

INGREDIENTS
Serves 4

2 tbsp sunflower oil
4 chicken leg portions
1 medium onion, peeled and
  chopped
1–2 garlic cloves, peeled and
  crushed
1 tbsp curry powder
25 g/1 oz butter
225 g/8 oz long-grain white
  rice

1 lemon, preferably unwaxed,
  sliced
600 ml/1 pint chicken stock
salt and freshly ground black
  pepper
2 tbsp flaked, toasted almonds
sprigs of fresh coriander, to
  garnish

1 Preheat the oven to 180°C/
350°F/Gas Mark 4, about
10 minutes before required. Heat
the oil in a large frying pan, add
the chicken legs and cook,
turning, until sealed and golden
all over. Using a slotted spoon,
remove from the pan and reserve.

2 Add the onion and garlic to
the oil remaining in the
frying pan and cook for 5–7
minutes, or until just beginning
to brown. Sprinkle in the curry
powder and cook, stirring, for a
further 1 minute. Return the
chicken to the pan and stir well,
then remove from the heat.

3 Melt the butter in a large
heavy-based saucepan. Add
the rice and cook, stirring, to
ensure that all the grains are
coated in the melted butter,
then remove from the heat.

4 Stir the lemon slices into the
chicken mixture, then spoon
the mixture onto the rice and
pour over the stock. Season to
taste with salt and pepper.

5 Cover with a tight-fitting lid
and cook in the preheated
oven for 45 minutes, or until
the rice is tender and the chicken
is cooked thoroughly. Serve
sprinkled with the toasted flaked
almonds and sprigs of coriander.

TASTY TIP

Choose a strength of curry
powder according to personal
taste. There is a huge range
of brands and mixtures available, from mild korma style
through to medium Madras
or hot vindaloo. Unless you
use spices frequently, buy
them in small quantities, as
they quickly become stale
and lose their flavour.
Store in clear glass jars in a
cool, dark place.

SCALLOP & POTATO GRATIN

INGREDIENTS   Serves 4

8 fresh scallops in their shells,
    cleaned
4 tbsp white wine
salt and freshly ground black
    pepper
50 g/2 oz butter
3 tbsp plain flour

2 tbsp single cream
50 g/2 oz Cheddar cheese,
    grated
450 g/1 lb potatoes, peeled
    and cut into chunks
1 tbsp milk

1 Preheat the oven to 220°C/ 425°F/Gas Mark 7. Clean 4 scallop shells to use as serving dishes and reserve. Place the scallops in a small saucepan with the wine, 150 ml/¼ pint water and salt and pepper. Cover and simmer very gently for 5 minutes, or until just tender. Remove with a slotted spoon and cut each scallop into 3 pieces. Reserve the cooking juices.

2 Melt 25 g/1 oz of the butter in a saucepan, stir in the flour and cook for 1 minute, stirring, then gradually whisk in the reserved cooking juices. Simmer, stirring, for 3–4 minutes until the sauce has thickened. Season to taste with salt and pepper. Remove from the heat and stir in the cream and 25 g/1 oz of the grated cheese. Fold in the scallops.

3 Boil the potatoes in lightly salted water until tender, then mash with the remaining butter and milk. Spoon or pipe the mashed potato around the edges of the cleaned scallop shells.

4 Divide the scallop mixture between the 4 shells, placing the mixture neatly in the centre. Sprinkle with the remaining grated cheese and bake in the preheated oven for about 10–15 minutes until golden brown and bubbling. Serve immediately.

HELPFUL HINT

You can ask your fishmonger to open and clean the scallops if you plan to cook them on the same day. Alternatively, buy scallops live and keep in the refrigerator for up to 24 hours. The simplest and safest way to open scallops is to place them flat side up on a baking sheet and put in a hot oven for a few minutes. Prise open the 2 shells and remove the white scallop meat and the bright orange coral.

WARM POTATO, PEAR & PECAN SALAD

INGREDIENTS

Serves 4

900 g/2 lb new potatoes,
    preferably red-skinned,
    unpeeled
salt and freshly ground black
    pepper
1 tsp Dijon mustard
2 tsp white wine vinegar

3 tbsp groundnut oil
1 tbsp hazelnut or walnut oil
2 tsp poppy seeds
2 firm ripe dessert pears
2 tsp lemon juice
175 g/6 oz baby spinach leaves
75 g/3 oz toasted pecan nuts

1 Scrub the potatoes, then cook in a saucepan of lightly salted boiling water for 15 minutes, or until tender. Drain, cut into halves, or quarters if large, and place in a serving bowl.

2 In a small bowl or jug, whisk together the mustard and vinegar. Gradually add the oils until the mixture begins to thicken. Stir in the poppy seeds and season to taste with salt and pepper.

3 Pour about two-thirds of the dressing over the hot potatoes and toss gently to coat. Leave until the potatoes have soaked up the dressing and are just warm.

4 Meanwhile, quarter and core the pears. Cut into thin slices, then sprinkle with the lemon juice to prevent them from going brown. Add to the potatoes with the spinach leaves and toasted pecan nuts. Gently mix together.

5 Drizzle the remaining dressing over the salad. Serve immediately before the spinach starts to wilt.

HANDY HINT

To toast the pecan nuts, place on a baking tray in a single layer and cook in a preheated oven at 180°C/350°F/Gas Mark 4 for 5 minutes, or under a medium grill for 3–4 minutes, turning frequently. Watch them carefully – they burn easily. If you can not get red-skinned new potatoes for this dish, add colour by using red-skinned pears instead. Look out for *Red Bartlett*, *Red Williams* and *Napolian*.

HERBED HASSELBACK POTATOES WITH ROAST CHICKEN

INGREDIENTS   Serves 4

8 medium, evenly-sized
  potatoes, peeled
3 large sprigs of fresh rosemary
1 tbsp oil
salt and freshly ground black
  pepper
350 g/12 oz baby parsnips,
  peeled

350 g/12 oz baby carrots,
  peeled
350 g/12 oz baby leeks,
  trimmed
75 g/3 oz butter
finely grated rind of 1 lemon,
  preferably unwaxed
1.6 kg/3½ lb chicken

1 Preheat the oven to 200°C/ 400°F/Gas Mark 6, about 15 minutes before cooking. Place a chopstick on either side of a potato and, with a sharp knife, cut down through the potato until you reach the chopsticks; take care not to cut right through the potato. Repeat these cuts every 5 mm/¼ inch along the length of the potato. Carefully ease 2–4 of the slices apart and slip in a few rosemary sprigs. Repeat with remaining potatoes. Brush with the oil and season well with salt and pepper.

2 Place the seasoned potatoes in a large roasting tin. Add the parsnips, carrots and leeks to the potatoes in the tin, cover with a wire rack or trivet.

3 Beat the butter and lemon rind together and season to taste. Smear the chicken with the lemon butter and place on the rack over the vegetables.

4 Roast in the preheated oven for 1 hour 40 minutes, basting the chicken and vegetables occasionally, until cooked thoroughly. The juices should run clear when the thigh is pierced with a skewer. Place the cooked chicken on a warmed serving platter, arrange the roast vegetables around it and serve immediately.

FOOD FACT

Hasselback potatoes were named after the Stockholm restaurant of the same name. Using chopsticks is a great way of ensuring that you slice just far enough through the potatoes so that they fan out during cooking. The potatoes can be given an attractive golden finish by mixing ¼ tsp ground turmeric or paprika with the oil.

SPICED INDIAN ROAST POTATOES WITH CHICKEN

INGREDIENTS   Serves 4

700 g/1½ lb waxy potatoes, peeled and cut into large chunks

salt and freshly ground black pepper

4 tbsp sunflower oil

8 chicken drumsticks

1 large Spanish onion, peeled and roughly chopped

3 shallots, peeled and roughly chopped

2 large garlic cloves, peeled and crushed

1 red chilli

2 tsp fresh root ginger, peeled and finely grated

2 tsp ground cumin

2 tsp ground coriander

pinch of cayenne pepper

4 cardamom pods, crushed

sprigs of fresh coriander, to garnish

1 Preheat the oven to 190°C/375°F/Gas Mark 5, about 10 minutes before cooking. Parboil the potatoes for 5 minutes in lightly salted boiling water, then drain thoroughly and reserve. Heat the oil in a large frying pan, add the chicken drumsticks and cook until sealed on all sides. Remove and reserve.

2 Add the onions and shallots to the pan and fry for 4–5 minutes, or until softened. Stir in the garlic, chilli and ginger and cook for 1 minute, stirring constantly. Stir in the ground cumin, coriander, cayenne pepper and crushed cardamom pods and continue to cook, stirring, for a further minute.

3 Add the potatoes to the pan, then add the chicken. Season to taste with salt and pepper. Stir gently until the potatoes and chicken pieces are coated in the onion and spice mixture.

4 Spoon into a large roasting tin and roast in the preheated oven for 35 minutes, or until the chicken and potatoes are cooked thoroughly. Garnish with fresh coriander and serve immediately.

HANDY HINT

Spanish onions are the largest white onions and they have a much milder flavour than smaller English ones. When frying onions, as in this recipe, do not be tempted to chop them in a food processor as this will make them too wet, and as a result the onions will steam rather than fry.

SPECIAL ROSTI

INGREDIENTS   Serves 4

700 g/1½ lb potatoes, scrubbed
but not peeled
salt and freshly ground black
pepper
75 g/3 oz butter
1 large onion, peeled and
finely chopped
1 garlic clove, peeled and
crushed

2 tbsp freshly chopped parsley
1 tbsp olive oil
75 g/3 oz Parma ham, thinly
sliced
50 g/2 oz sun-dried tomatoes,
chopped
175 g/ 6 oz Emmenthal cheese,
grated
mixed green salad, to serve

1 Cook the potatoes in a large saucepan of salted boiling water for about 10 minutes, until just tender. Drain in a colander, then rinse in cold water. Drain again. Leave until cool enough to handle, then peel off the skins.

2 Melt the butter in a large frying pan and gently fry the onion and garlic for about 3 minutes until softened and beginning to colour. Remove from the heat.

3 Coarsely grate the potatoes into a large bowl, then stir in the onion and garlic mixture. Sprinkle over the parsley and stir well to mix. Season to taste with salt and pepper.

4 Heat the oil in the frying pan and cover the base of the pan with half the potato mixture. Lay the slices of Parma ham on top. Sprinkle with the chopped sun-dried tomatoes, then scatter the grated Emmenthal over the top.

5 Finally, top with the remaining potato mixture. Cook over a low heat, pressing down with a palette knife from time to time, for 10–15 minutes, or until the bottom is golden brown. Carefully invert the rosti onto a large plate, then carefully slide back into the pan and cook the other side until golden. Serve cut into wedges with a mixed green salad.

HELPFUL HINT

To make sure the rosti is the right thickness, you will need a heavy-based non-stick frying pan with a diameter of about 23 cm/9 inches.

MEDITERRANEAN POTATO SALAD

INGREDIENTS

Serves 4

700 g/1½ lb small waxy
  potatoes
2 red onions, peeled and
  roughly chopped
1 yellow pepper, deseeded
  and roughly chopped
1 green pepper, deseeded and
  roughly chopped
6 tbsp extra-virgin olive oil
125 g/4 oz ripe tomatoes,
  chopped

50 g/2 oz pitted black olives,
  sliced
125 g/4 oz feta cheese
3 tbsp freshly chopped parsley
2 tbsp white wine vinegar
1 tsp Dijon mustard
1 tsp clear honey
salt and freshly ground black
  pepper
sprigs of fresh parsley, to
  garnish

1 Preheat the oven to 200°C/
400°F/Gas Mark 6. Place the
potatoes in a large saucepan of
salted water, bring to the boil and
simmer until just tender. Do not
overcook. Drain and plunge into
cold water, to stop them from
cooking further.

2 Place the onions in a bowl
with the yellow and green
peppers, then pour over 2
tablespoons of the olive oil. Stir
and spoon onto a large baking
tray. Cook in the preheated oven
for 25–30 minutes, or until the
vegetables are tender and lightly
charred in places, stirring
occasionally. Remove from the
oven and transfer to a large bowl.

3 Cut the potatoes into bite-
sized pieces and mix with the
roasted onions and peppers. Add
the tomatoes and olives to the
potatoes. Crumble over the feta

cheese and sprinkle with
the chopped parsley.

4 Whisk together the remaining
olive oil, vinegar, mustard
and honey, then season to taste
with salt and pepper. Pour the
dressing over the potatoes and
toss gently together. Garnish
with parsley sprigs and serve
immediately.

FOOD FACT

Tomatoes are such an integral
part of many cuisines, that it
is hard to believe they were
only introduced to Europe
from the Americas a few
hundred years ago. There are
lots of new flavoursome
varieties now available to try.
Those sold still attached to
the vine tend to have a
particularly good flavour.

POTATO & GOATS' CHEESE TART

INGREDIENTS   Serves 6

275 g/10 oz prepared
  shortcrust pastry, thawed
  if frozen
550 g/1¼ lb small waxy
  potatoes
salt and freshly ground black
  pepper
beaten egg, for brushing
2 tbsp sun-dried tomato paste

¼ tsp chilli powder, or to taste
1 large egg
150 ml/¼ pint soured cream
150 ml/¼ pint milk
2 tbsp freshly snipped chives
300 g/11 oz goats' cheese,
  sliced
salad and warm crusty bread,
  to serve

1 Preheat the oven to 190°C/ 375°F/Gas Mark 5, about 10 minutes before cooking. Roll the pastry out on a lightly floured surface and use to line a 23 cm/ 9 inch fluted flan tin. Chill in the refrigerator for 30 minutes.

2 Scrub the potatoes, place in a large saucepan of lightly salted water and bring to the boil. Simmer for 10–15 minutes, or until the potatoes are tender. Drain and reserve until cool enough to handle.

3 Line the pastry case with greaseproof paper and baking beans or crumpled tinfoil and bake blind in the preheated oven for 15 minutes. Remove from the oven and discard the paper and beans or tinfoil. Brush the base with a little beaten egg, then return to the oven and cook for a further 5 minutes. Remove from the oven.

4 Cut the potatoes into 1 cm/ ½ inch thick slices; reserve.

Spread the sun-dried tomato paste over the base of pastry case, sprinkle with the chilli powder, then arrange the potato slices on top in a decorative pattern.

5 Beat together the egg, soured cream, milk and chives, then season to taste with salt and pepper. Pour over the potatoes. Arrange the goats' cheese on top of the potatoes. Bake in the preheated oven for 30 minutes until golden brown and set. Serve immediately with salad and warm bread.

HELPFUL HINT

Using bought ready-made shortcrust pastry is a good way to save time, but always remove it from the refrigerator 10–15 minutes before rolling out, otherwise it may be difficult to handle. Brushing the base with egg helps seal the pastry and keeps it crisp when filled.

POTATO PANCAKES WITH SMOKED SALMON

INGREDIENTS   Serves 4

450 g/1 lb floury potatoes,
   peeled and quartered
salt and freshly ground black
   pepper
1 large egg
1 large egg yolk
25 g/1 oz butter
25 g/1 oz plain flour
150 ml/¼ pint double cream
2 tbsp freshly chopped parsley

5 tbsp crème fraîche
1 tbsp horseradish sauce
225 g/8 oz smoked salmon,
   sliced
salad leaves, to serve

TO GARNISH:
lemon slices
snipped chives

1 Cook the potatoes in a sauce-pan of lightly salted boiling water for 15–20 minutes, or until tender. Drain thoroughly, then mash until free of lumps. Beat in the whole egg and egg yolk, together with the butter. Beat until smooth and creamy. Slowly beat in the flour and cream, then season to taste with salt and pepper. Stir in the chopped parsley.

2 Beat the crème fraîche and horseradish sauce together in a small bowl, cover with cling-film and reserve.

3 Heat a lightly oiled, heavy-based frying pan over a medium-high heat. Place a few spoonfuls of the potato mixture in the hot pan and cook for 4–5 minutes, or until cooked and golden, turning halfway through cooking time. Remove from the pan, drain on absorbent kitchen paper and keep warm. Repeat with the remaining mixture.

4 Arrange the pancakes on individual serving plates. Place the smoked salmon on the pancakes and spoon over a little of the horseradish sauce. Serve with salad and the remaining horseradish sauce and garnish with lemon slices and chives.

TASTY TIP

Horseradish is a pungent root, usually finely grated and mixed with oil and vinegar or cream to make horseradish sauce. Commercially-made sauces vary in hotness, so it is best to add a little at a time to the crème fraîche and taste until you have the desired flavour.

SALMON WITH HERBED POTATOES

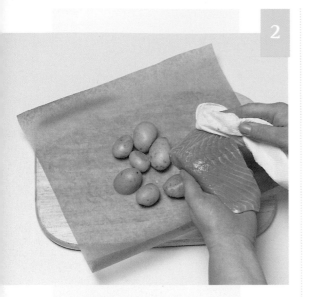

INGREDIENTS   Serves 4

450 g/1 lb baby new potatoes
salt and freshly ground black
  pepper
4 salmon steaks, each
  weighing about 175 g/6 oz
1 carrot, peeled and cut into
  fine strips
175 g/6 oz asparagus spears,
  trimmed

175 g/6 oz sugar snap peas,
  trimmed
finely grated rind and juice 1
  lemon
25 g/1 oz butter
4 large sprigs of fresh parsley

1 Preheat the oven to 190°C/ 375°F/Gas Mark 5, about 10 minutes before required. Parboil the potatoes in lightly salted boiling water for 5–8 minutes until they are barely tender. Drain and reserve.

2 Cut out 4 pieces of baking parchment paper, measuring 20.5 cm/8 inches square, and place on the work surface. Arrange the parboiled potatoes on top. Wipe the salmon steaks and place on top of the potatoes.

3 Place the carrot strips in a bowl with the asparagus spears, sugar snaps and grated lemon rind and juice. Season to taste with salt and pepper. Toss lightly together.

4 Divide the vegetables evenly between the salmon. Dot the top of each parcel with butter and a sprig of parsley.

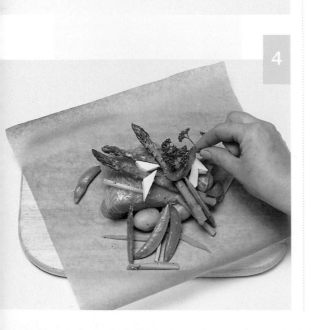

5 To wrap a parcel, lift up 2 opposite sides of the paper and fold the edges together. Twist the paper at the other 2 ends to seal the parcel well. Repeat with the remaining parcels.

6 Place the parcels on a baking tray and bake in the preheated oven for 15 minutes. Place an unopened parcel on each plate and open just before eating.

HELPFUL HINT

Cooking fish *en papillote* is an excellent way of keeping in all the juices, flavour and aroma of the fish and vegetables. Your guests will also enjoy the anticipation of opening these surprise packages. Do let the parcels stand for a few minutes before serving as the steam can be burning hot when opened.

Lamb & Potato Moussaka

INGREDIENTS — Serves 4

700 g/1½ lb cooked roast lamb

700 g/1½ lb potatoes, peeled

125 g/4 oz butter

1 large onion, peeled and chopped

2–4 garlic cloves, peeled and crushed

3 tbsp tomato purée

1 tbsp freshly chopped parsley

salt and freshly ground black pepper

3–4 tbsp olive oil

2 medium aubergines, trimmed and sliced

4 medium tomatoes, sliced

2 medium eggs

300 ml/½ pint Greek yogurt

2–3 tbsp Parmesan cheese, grated

1 Preheat the oven to 200°C/ 400°F/Gas Mark 6, about 15 minutes before required. Trim the lamb, discarding any fat then cut into fine dice and reserve. Thinly slice the potatoes and rinse thoroughly in cold water, then pat dry with a clean tea towel.

2 Melt 50 g/2 oz of the butter in a frying pan and fry the potatoes, in batches, until crisp and golden. Using a slotted spoon, remove from the pan and reserve. Use a third of the potatoes to line the base of an ovenproof dish.

3 Add the onion and garlic to the butter remaining in the pan and cook for 5 minutes. Add the lamb and fry for 1 minute. Blend the tomato purée with 3 tablespoons of water and stir into the pan with the parsley and salt and pepper. Spoon over the layer of potatoes, then top with the remaining potato slices.

4 Heat the oil and the remaining butter in the pan and brown the aubergine slices for 5–6 minutes. Arrange the tomatoes on top of the potatoes, then the aubergines on top of the tomatoes. Beat the eggs with the yogurt and Parmesan cheese and pour over the aubergine and tomatoes. Bake in the preheated oven for 25 minutes, or until golden and piping hot. Serve.

HANDY HINT

It is worth salting the aubergines to ensure that any bitterness is removed. Layer the slices in a colander, sprinkling a little salt between the layers. Leave for 20 minutes, then rinse under cold running water and pat dry on absorbent kitchen paper. Salting helps the aubergines to absorb less oil when frying.

CROWN ROAST OF LAMB

INGREDIENTS   Serves 6

1 lamb crown roast
salt and freshly ground black
  pepper
1 tbsp sunflower oil
1 small onion, peeled and
  finely chopped
2–3 garlic cloves, peeled and
  crushed
2 celery stalks, trimmed and
  finely chopped
125 g/4 oz cooked mixed
  basmati and wild rice

75 g/3 oz ready-to-eat-dried
  apricots, chopped
50 g/2 oz pine nuts, toasted
1 tbsp finely grated orange
  rind
2 tbsp freshly chopped
  coriander
1 small egg, beaten
freshly roasted potatoes and
  green vegetables, to serve

1 Preheat the oven to 180°C/ 350°F/Gas Mark 4, about 10 minutes before roasting. Wipe the crown roast and season the cavity with salt and pepper. Place in a roasting tin and cover the ends of the bones with small pieces of tinfoil.

2 Heat the oil in a small saucepan and cook the onion, garlic and celery for 5 minutes, then remove the saucepan from the heat. Add the cooked rice with the apricots, pine nuts, orange rind and coriander. Season with salt and pepper, then stir in the egg and mix well.

3 Carefully spoon the prepared stuffing into the cavity of the lamb, then roast in the preheated oven for 1–1½ hours. Remove the lamb from the oven and remove and discard the tinfoil from the bones. Return to the oven and continue to cook for a further 15 minutes, or until cooked to personal preference.

4 Remove from the oven and leave to rest for 10 minutes before serving with the roast potatoes and freshly cooked vegetables.

FOOD FACT

Best end of neck consists of 6–7 small chops. Crown roast is made by joining 2 best ends together, making a perfect central cavity to fill with stuffing. When ready to serve, the trimmed cutlet bones may be topped, if liked, with paper frills, looking like tiny chefs' hats.

TERIYAKI BEEF

INGREDIENTS   Serves 4

550 g/1¼ lb rump or sirloin
   steak
1 medium onion, peeled and
   finely sliced
5 cm/2 inch piece of fresh root
   ginger, peeled and coarsely
   chopped
1 bird's-eye chilli, deseeded
   and finely chopped
6 tbsp light soy sauce

2 tbsp sake or sweet sherry
1 tbsp lemon juice
1 tsp clear honey
250 g/9 oz glutinous rice
sunflower oil, for spraying

TO GARNISH:
carrot matchsticks
daikon matchsticks
sprigs of fresh coriander

1 Trim the steak, discarding
any fat or gristle, and place
in a non-metallic shallow dish.
Scatter the sliced onion over the
steak. Mix the ginger with the
chilli and sprinkle over the steak
and onion.

2 Blend the soy sauce
with the sake or sherry,
the lemon juice and honey.
Stir well, then pour over the
steak and onion. Cover and
leave to marinate in the
refrigerator for at least 1 hour,
longer if time permits. Turn
the steak over, or occasionally
spoon the marinade over
the meat, during this time.

3 Place the rice in a saucepan
with 450 ml/¾ pint of water
and cook for 15 minutes, or
until tender. Drain if necessary,
then pack into 4 warmed oiled
individual moulds. Quickly
invert onto 4 individual warm
plates and keep warm.

4 Spray or brush a griddle pan
with oil, then heat until
really hot. Drain the steak and
cook in the griddle pan for 2–3
minutes on each side, or until
cooked to personal preference.
Remove from the pan and slice
thinly. Arrange on the warm
serving plates, garnish with the
carrot and daikon matchsticks
and coriander sprigs, then serve.

FOOD FACT

There are more than 200
different types of chillies. The
heat comes from capsaicin, a
compound found in the
membranes and seeds and,
to a lesser extent, in the flesh.
Chillies range in potency from
very mild to blisteringly hot.
Bird's-eye chillies, whether
red or green, are one of
the smallest and among
the hottest.

INDEX